MARY BERRY'S
QUICK & EASY
CAKES
· ·

MARY BERRY'S
QUICK & EASY
CAKES

BBC BOOKS

About the author

M ary Berry has written 24 cookery books which have sold a combined total of some 2½ million copies. Mary insists on the highest quality ingredients, and always produces practical and reliable recipes that work. She takes great care to give careful explanations for these recipes that ensure success every time.

Mary has made numerous television and radio appearances. She lives in Buckinghamshire from where she currently runs aga cookery workshops.

Acknowledgements

I would like to thank Fiona Oyston for all her hard work on this book. Her tremendous enthusiasm for the subject and meticulous attention to detail have proved a tower of strength to me.

Published by BBC Books,
a division of BBC Enterprises Limited,
Woodlands, 80 Wood Lane, London W12 0TT

First published 1993
© Mary Berry 1993

ISBN 0 563 36786 5

Designed by *Peter Bridgewater*
Photographs by *James Murphy*
Illustrations by *Lorraine Harrison*
Styling by *Jane McLeish*
Home Economist *Allyson Birch*

Typeset by Create Publishing Services, Bath, Avon
Printed and bound in Great Britain by Clays Ltd, St Ives plc
Colour Separations by Technik Ltd, Berkhamsted
Cover printed by Clays Ltd, St Ives plc

CONTENTS

INTRODUCTION 7

CAKE-MAKING STORE-CUPBOARD 8

CAKE-MAKING EQUIPMENT 11

TECHNIQUES AND TIPS 13

QUICK BREADS AND TEABREADS 17

LARGE CAKES AND SPONGE CAKES 25

BISCUITS AND COOKIES 37

FAMILY CAKES 45

CHOCOLATE CAKES 53

LITTLE CAKES AND SCONES 63

CAKES FOR DESSERT 75

FAST CHEESECAKES 83

TRAYBAKES 93

NO-BAKE CAKES 105

CAKES THAT CHILDREN ENJOY MOST 113

WHOLEFOOD CAKES 123

INDEX 133

INTRODUCTION

G reat news! Most of the recipes in this book take no more than 15 minutes to prepare and they are fast and simple to finish too. There is no place for complicated icings or fiddly techniques. These recipes are made and finished with speed and are every bit as delicious as cakes made by old-fashioned methods.

Cakes and biscuits have long been part of our traditional diet, there is no need to eat cakes everyday but it is good to have them in the tin or in the freezer for when they are wanted.

I am a firm believer in using only the very best and the freshest ingredients for home baking. The major ingredients used in cake-making such as flour, butter, eggs, nuts and fruit provide essential nutrients and should be enjoyed as part of a sensibly balanced diet.

HOW TO FOLLOW A CAKE RECIPE

This seems very obvious but not following a recipe closely is often the reason why a cake goes wrong. For the quickest and most successful results read the recipe through carefully, checking that you have all the ingredients in the store-cupboard. Then put the oven on, prepare the tin and weigh out the ingredients accurately.

Check that you have time to make and bake the cake. It is so easy to begin with good intentions, only to be interrupted and then it's time to collect the children from school! Check also to see if icings can be made ahead.

NOTES ON THE RECIPES

- Follow either metric or imperial measures for the recipes, not a mixture of both.
- Unless specified otherwise:
  - spoon measures are level
  - eggs are size 3
  - white flour is used.

CAKE-MAKING
STORE-CUPBOARD

The best quality ingredients are needed to make cakes that taste as fresh and as good as possible.

BUTTER AND MARGARINE

It is not necessary always to use butter to obtain the best results. Indeed, the flavour of butter would be masked where strong flavours are used, such as in a chocolate cake, but butter must be used where the flavour is all-important, for instance in shortbread.

Soft margarines have improved greatly and now have a good flavour, and cakes made with them have excellent keeping qualities.

Whatever brand of margarine you choose, always check the side of the packet for any instructions. It is all too easy to pick up a low-fat spread by mistake, these are not suitable for baking because of their high water content. Please make doubly sure that you are using the right margarine, and you will avoid the awful disappointment of baking something that doesn't work.

FLOUR

Although many types of baking flours are available I suggest only plain and self-raising flour are used for cakes. Special cake flours are available too but the formula varies so you may not find the results they give so reliable. In the 'healthier' cakes I've used self-raising brown flour.

For bread-making strong flour is better.

RAISING AGENTS

The baking powders which are on the market today contain a slower-acting raising agent which is more tolerant if mixtures are made up and left before baking. If it is more convenient, you can always make the cake mixture and then bake it later.

Along with baking powder, it is useful, but not essential, to have bicarbonate of soda and cream of tartar in the store-cupboard.

EGGS

Size 3 eggs are used in the recipes unless otherwise specified. If your kitchen is warm keep the eggs in the fridge, but bring them out to come to room temperature before using them.

SUGAR

Use natural sugars such as golden granulated and golden caster sugar where possible, the flavour is so much better. Soft light brown or muscovado sugar is also excellent, but be careful with dark muscovado sugar as it easily overpowers other flavours. The coarser demerara sugar is useful for sprinkling on top of cakes and also to add crunch to cheesecake bases.

CHOCOLATE

Cocoa powder is by far the cheapest and best way of obtaining a good chocolate flavour in baking.

Bournville chocolate is excellent where real chocolate is needed, there is no need to use the expensive dessert chocolate.

Chocolate-flavoured cake covering is not a patch on the real thing but is useful to make quick chocolate curls.

FRUIT AND NUTS

Nuts are expensive and have a short shelf life, quickly going rancid in a warm kitchen. However, you can use the freezer as an extra store-cupboard. Whole shelled nuts keep for up to five years in the freezer, flaked and ground almonds for one year. Shake out only what is required and pop the remainder back.

Dried fruit can also dry out if left for too long in a warm kitchen so you can freeze it in polythene bags. I also recommend using ready-soaked dried apricots and prunes to save the soaking time.

OTHER INGREDIENTS

Lemon juice   Where lemon juice is required, do use fresh lemon juice if possible as it will give the best flavour.

Gelatine   You can buy the powder in 15 g (½ oz) packets in boxes.

Easy-blend dried yeast   This greatly speeds up dough-making. It is a fast-acting dried yeast which is simply mixed into the dry flour.

Golden syrup   Should the sugar in the syrup become crystallized, just gently warm it and it will become runny again.

Black treacle   This is used to give a richer colour and flavour to Christmas cakes, gingerbreads and parkins.

Spices   The most useful to keep in store are ground cinnamon, ground mixed spice, ground ginger and whole nutmeg. Ground spices are best kept in the dark to preserve the colour.

Glacé cherries   These usually have a thick syrup in the centre, so it is best to halve or quarter them, rinse under the running tap and thoroughly dry them before use, otherwise they may sink to the bottom of the cake.

Candied peel   This is apt to dry out if kept on the larder shelf, so slip the tub into a polythene bag and keep it in the freezer for next time. Part-thaw before using.

CAKE-MAKING EQUIPMENT

BASIC ESSENTIALS

Specialist equipment is not necessary for cake-making but there are a few basic essentials which help to make life so much easier.

Good, solid cake tins and baking trays are worth the initial investment as they will last you a lifetime. If you need more, scan the local jumble sales and car boot sales. Loose-bottomed cake tins are useful but avoid the ones with thick insulated bases as they stop the cake cooking evenly in a modern cooker.

A palette knife is indispensable to both spread and smooth mixtures into tins or icings onto cakes, and also to lift biscuits off baking trays or loosen a cake from the sides of the tin before turning out.

Plastic or rubber cake scrapers are useful to get all of the mixture out of the bowl and into the tin.

FOOD MIXERS AND PROCESSORS

Essential to the all-in-one method of cake-making is an electric whisk, although it doesn't matter whether it is hand-held or an electric food mixer. A wire balloon whisk is also useful for small quantities of egg yolks, whites or cream.

A food processor is very much a time saver, but it is all too easy to over-process the mixture. Use the pulse button where available to give you more control.

Fruit and nuts can easily be chopped in a processor but always mix them into the mixture by hand.

Processors are also excellent for making breadcrumbs and for mixing pastry or biscuit doughs. In bread-making they can even do the time- and effort-consuming kneading for you.

CHOOSING AND PREPARING TINS

Choosing the correct size of cake tin for the recipe is of paramount importance. So often a cake fails simply because the cake tin was the wrong size.

Loose-bottomed cake tins are excellent for cake-making. There is no need to line them, simply grease the base and sides and the cake will be easy to turn out. The base of tins without a loose bottom do need to be lined with greased greaseproof paper. For a rich cake mixture such as a rich fruit cake, the base and sides of the tin need to be lined as well as greased.

I have used spring release tins for the cheesecakes in the book but they are not essential. You could use lined loose-bottomed round cake tins instead. You need to line the loose-bottomed tins because often the cheesecake mixture is runny before cooking and so would run out. (see 'Lining Tins' on page 13.)

I find melted white vegetable fat by far the best to grease tins. Use a pastry brush to brush the melted fat evenly all over the tin.

TINS AND EQUIPMENT USED IN THIS BOOK

- *18-cm (7-inch) shallow square tin* for flapjacks, toffee and bars
- *2 × 18-cm (7-inch) sandwich tins; 2 × 20-cm (8-inch) sandwich tins* for sponges
- *18-cm (7-inch) deep round cake tin; 20-cm (8-inch) deep round cake tin; 23-cm (9-inch) deep round cake tin* for fruit, cherry and richer cakes
- *30 × 23-cm (12 × 9-inch) roasting tin* for traybakes; *33 × 23-cm (13 × 9-inch) Swiss roll tin*
- *450-g (1-lb) loaf tin; 900-g (2-lb) loaf tin* for all loaves and teabreads
- *18-cm (7-inch) spring release tin; 20-cm (8-inch) spring release tin; 23-cm (9-inch) spring release tin* for cheesecakes
- *2 bun tins; 2–3 large, solid, flat baking trays; cooling rack; set of plastic measuring spoons; biscuit cutters, plain and fluted; (griddle) or heavy-based frying-pan*

OVENS

Regrettably, no two ovens are the same whether they are gas, electric or fan-assisted. Particular care is needed with the timing of fan ovens as they can all too quickly dry out a cake by overcooking.

All of the recipes in this book were tested in a conventional oven. Reduce the oven temperature accordingly for a fan oven (following the manufacturer's instructions).

It is always a good idea to treat any cookery book as a working manual. In pencil jot down beside each recipe the exact time it took to cook in *your* oven. If the time varies enormously, then you could check your oven with an oven thermometer.

Unless specified otherwise, always cook cakes in the centre of the oven. Glance at the cake about three-quarters of the way through the cooking time to see if it is done.

LINING TINS

BASES

Most cakes require only the bases to be greased and lined with greased greaseproof paper. Whatever the shape of the tin, place the base of the tin on the greaseproof paper, draw around it in pencil, then cut out just inside the pencil line.

If you do a lot of baking it is worth cutting out several bases at once and storing them flat in a polythene bag for future use.

SIDES

Where a rich cake mixture is used, like a rich fruit cake, it is necessary to line the sides of the tin as well as the base. Cut a strip (or 2 strips if necessary) of greaseproof paper long enough to reach around the tin and overlap slightly, and high enough to extend about 2.5 cm (1 inch) above the top of the tin. Fold the bottom edge of the strip up by about 2.5 cm (1 inch) creasing it firmly. Open out the fold and cut slanting lines into this narrow strip at intervals (Diagram 1). Fit this strip into the greased tin, where the snipped edge will enable the paper to fit snugly into the base of any shaped tin. Fit the base disc over the cut part of the paper (Diagram 2) and the tin is then fully lined.

FOLD

DIAGRAM 1   DIAGONAL CUTS

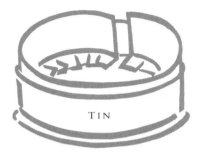

TIN

DIAGRAM 2

If time is short, turn the tin to be lined upside down and mould a piece of foil over the top. Use this to line the tin and grease well.

ALL-IN-ONE METHOD

The all-in-one method means just that. All of the main ingredients go into the bowl at the same time to be mixed. The fat must be soft baking margarine.

FAT

It is essential to use a soft baking margarine which is of the correct consistency even when taken straight from the fridge. Butter and block margarines do not work successfully for this method as they are too hard to be blended easily with the remaining ingredients.

RAISING AGENT

In the all-in-one method self-raising flour and baking powder are used together to give the cake the necessary lift. The quickness of the method means that there is not so much air beaten into the mixture as there would be if making the cake the traditional way. Don't be tempted to use more baking powder than specified or the cake will rise up and then sink back again.

TESTING TO SEE IF A CAKE IS COOKED

Most cakes are cooked when the cake begins to shrink away from the sides of the tin and when the cake springs back after being pressed lightly with the finger. The look of the cake gives an idea too. See each individual recipe for advice.

For fruit cakes, push a skewer into the centre of the cake, if it is done the skewer should come out clean. If cakes look as though they're browning too much on the top before the inside is cooked, cover the top loosely with foil.

PIPING

This can make all the difference to the finish of a cake, particularly if it is for a special occasion, and you don't need to have a vast array of piping bags and nozzles to achieve a good result. Strong plastic piping bags can be used and washed over and over again and a plain, small star and large star nozzle are all you need.

FILLING A PIPING BAG

Stand the bag and nozzle point down in a jug and then fold the top edges of the bag over the top of the jug. That way it is much easier to spoon the cream or icing into the bag without getting it all over yourself!

PIPING CHOCOLATE

A quick and easy way to pipe chocolate is to place the melted chocolate into 2 polythene bags which have been put together for strength, snip off the corner and then simply drizzle the chocolate over the cake.

Alternatively, make a greaseproof paper piping bag, by following the diagrams shown below.

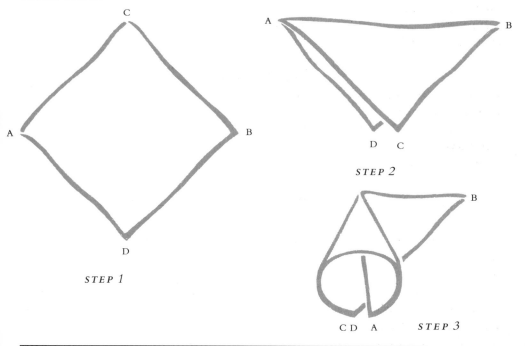

STEP 1

STEP 2

STEP 3

TOASTING NUTS

The best way to toast nuts, such as flaked almonds, is under the grill but they do need to be watched very carefully. You need to turn them frequently with a long handled palette knife to obtain a good even colour and also to prevent them from burning.

Coconut is also best toasted in this way but be warned, it browns and then burns very quickly.

Whole hazelnuts are best browned in the oven to remove their skins. Rub them briskly in a tea towel to remove the skins, returning any nuts with stubborn skins to the oven for a little longer if necessary.

STORING AND FREEZING CAKES AND BAKES

In general, few cakes improve with keeping except perhaps sticky gingerbread, Yorkshire parkin and of course rich fruit cakes.

Lighter fruit cakes and sponge cakes are definitely best eaten soon after making but they can be kept fresh for a short time in an airtight tin or box, or wrapped in foil or cling film.

A rich fruit cake which is being stored for a few months must be wrapped in greaseproof paper and then foil to prevent the acid in the fruit corroding the foil.

Make sure that cakes and biscuits are not stored in the same tin, as the moisture from the cake will make the biscuits soggy.

Most cakes can be frozen either whole or in pieces, well wrapped in foil, cling film or polythene bags. Don't freeze cakes for more than 3 months or they will lose their flavour.

QUICK BREADS
AND TEABREADS

Nothing can beat the aroma of freshly baked bread and bread-making no longer needs to be a lengthy process. Fast-acting, easy-blend dried yeast is much quicker and simpler to use than fresh or ordinary dried yeast. It does not need to be reconstituted in liquid first but is simply mixed into the dry flour.

Teabreads make a delicious addition to the tea table and are also quick to make, using the all-in-one or rubbed-in methods. Usually made with nuts or fruit added, teabreads are best served fresh, sliced and thickly buttered.

QUICK GRANARY ROLLS

MAKES

—— 12 ——

*350 g (12 oz) strong white
    flour*
350 g (12 oz) granary flour
1 ½ teaspoons salt
1 ½ teaspoons sugar
*1 sachet easy-blend dried
    yeast*
40 g (1 ½ oz) margarine
*About 450 ml (15 fl oz)
    tepid milk and water
    mixed*

To make a close-textured, more substantial roll you could use all granary flour. To glaze the rolls, brush the dough with a little milk and sprinkle with cracked wheat just before baking them.

Lightly grease 2 baking trays. Put the dry ingredients and the margarine into a food processor and process briefly to mix in the margarine. Or, rub the margarine into the dry ingredients by hand.

Add the milk and water mixture in a continuous stream through the feed tube, while the processor is running, and mix the ingredients to a dough. Process for a further 2 minutes to knead the dough. Or, add the liquid to the dry ingredients, mix well and then knead thoroughly until smooth and elastic.

Turn the dough out onto a floured surface and divide into 12 even pieces. Shape each piece into a round and place on a baking tray, allowing room for expansion.

Cover the rolls with oiled cling film and place in a warm place to prove until they are doubled in size. Pre-heat the oven to gas mark 7, 425°F (220°C).

Uncover the rolls and bake for about 10–15 minutes, until they have browned on top and sound hollow when the base is tapped. Lift onto a wire rack to cool.

ENGLISH MUFFINS

M A K E S

—— about 14 ——

These old-fashioned English muffins are traditionally pulled apart, not cut, through the middle and eaten warm with lashings of butter. Any left over will store for 2–3 days in an airtight container and are then best split in half and eaten toasted.

Put the dry ingredients into a food processor and mix quickly. With the processor on, add the tepid milk in a continuous stream through the feed tube to mix the ingredients to a dough. Blend for a further 1 minute to knead the mixture. Alternatively, mix the ingredients by hand and knead until smooth and elastic. Turn the dough out onto a lightly floured surface and roll out to a thickness of about 1 cm (½ inch) with a floured rolling pin.

Cut the dough into rounds using a 7.5-cm (3-inch) plain cutter, place on a well-floured baking sheet and dust the tops with the semolina. Cover loosely and leave in a warm place until doubled in size (approximately 1 hour).

Lightly oil a griddle or heavy-based frying-pan and place on the hob to heat. Cook the muffins in 2–3 batches for about 7 minutes each side, turning the heat down once the muffins go into the pan. When cooked they should be well risen and brown on both sides.

Cool slightly on a wire rack before splitting and buttering to serve.

INGREDIENTS

700 g (1 ½ lb) strong plain flour
2 teaspoons sugar
1 sachet easy-blend dried yeast
1 ½ teaspoons salt
450 ml (15 fl oz) tepid milk
1 teaspoon fine semolina for dusting

IRISH SODA BREAD

———— • ————

450 g (1 lb) plain brown
  flour
1 teaspoon bicarbonate of
  soda
1 teaspoon salt
300 ml (10 fl oz) buttermilk
  or 150 ml (5 fl oz) milk
  and 150 ml (5 fl oz)
  natural yoghurt, mixed
About 6 tablespoons tepid
  water

Rolled oats can be added to give the bread more texture. Simply replace 50 g (2 oz) of the flour with the same quantity of oats. Soda bread is best eaten on the day of making.

Pre-heat the oven to gas mark 6, 400°F (200°C). Lightly grease a baking tray.

Mix together the dry ingredients in a mixing bowl. Add the buttermilk (or milk and yoghurt mixture) and tepid water and mix to form a very soft dough.

Turn the dough out onto a lightly floured surface and shape into a neat round about 18 cm (7 inches) in diameter. Place on the baking tray and make a shallow cross in the top. Bake for 30 minutes, then turn the bread upside-down and continue cooking for about a further 10–15 minutes, or until the bread sounds hollow when tapped on the bottom.

Cool on a wire rack.

ALL-BRAN FRUIT LOAF

—— • ——

This fruit loaf couldn't be easier but you do need to start the night before.

Place the All-Bran, sugar, fruit and milk in a bowl. Stir thoroughly to mix, cover and leave in a cool place to soak overnight.

The next day, pre-heat the oven to gas mark 4, 350°F (180°C). Grease and base line a 900-g (2-lb) loaf tin with greased greaseproof paper.

Stir the beaten egg into the soaked mixture, and then sift in the flour and spice. Mix thoroughly and spoon into the prepared tin. Bake for about 1–1¼ hours, or until a skewer inserted into the centre comes out clean. Loosely cover the loaf with foil if it starts to brown too much near the end of the cooking time.

Allow to cool in the tin for 10 minutes, then turn out onto a wire rack to cool. Serve sliced and buttered.

INGREDIENTS

100 g (4 oz) All-Bran breakfast cereal
50 g (2 oz) light muscovado sugar
275 g (10 oz) mixed dried fruit
300 ml (10 fl oz) milk
1 egg, beaten
100 g (4 oz) self-raising flour
½ teaspoon mixed spice

BORROWDALE TEABREAD

—— • ——

INGREDIENTS

100 g (4 oz) sultanas
100 g (4 oz) currants
100 g (4 oz) raisins
475 ml (16 fl oz) strong tea,
* strained*
225 g (8 oz) dark
* muscovado sugar*
2 eggs
450 g (1 lb) self-raising
* brown flour*

A wonderful moist teabread to serve with butter. The fruit is soaked in tea overnight. Use tea left in the pot, either hot or cold. If you choose to make two 450-g (1-lb) loaves the cooking time will of course be shorter – about 30–40 minutes.

Place the sultanas, currants and raisins in a bowl with the tea, cover and leave to soak overnight.

Pre-heat the oven to gas mark 4, 350°F (180°C). Grease and base line a 900-g (2-lb) loaf tin with greased greaseproof paper. Mix the sugar and eggs together until light and fluffy. Add the flour with the soaked fruits and any remaining liquid and mix thoroughly together.

Spoon the mixture into the prepared loaf tin and level the surface. Bake for about 1 hour or until a skewer inserted into the centre comes out clean. Leave to cool in the tin.

Serve sliced and spread with butter.

SULTANA MALT LOAF

—— • ——

Malt extract can be found in health food shops. This loaf is best kept for 2 days before eating. The addition of the tea adds both colour and flavour.

INGREDIENTS

225 g (8 oz) plain flour
½ teaspoon bicarbonate of soda
1 teaspoon baking powder
225 g (8 oz) sultanas
50 g (2 oz) demerara sugar
175 g (6 oz) malt extract
1 tablespoon black treacle
2 eggs, beaten
150 ml (5 fl oz) black tea, strained
Demerara sugar for dusting

Pre-heat the oven to gas mark 2, 300°F (150°C). Grease and base line a 900-g (2-lb) loaf tin with greased greaseproof paper. Sift together the flour, bicarbonate of soda and the baking powder. Stir in the sultanas.

Gently heat the sugar, malt extract and black treacle together in a saucepan. Pour onto the dry ingredients with the beaten eggs and tea. Beat well until smooth.

Pour into the prepared tin and sprinkle the top with a little demerara sugar. Bake for about 1 ½ hours or until well risen and firm to the touch. Allow to cool for 10 minutes in the tin before turning out onto a wire rack to cool. Serve sliced and buttered.

CHEESE AND CELERY CROWN LOAF

•

INGREDIENTS

350 g (12 oz) self-raising
  white flour
40 g (1 ½ oz) soft margarine
Freshly ground black pepper
½ teaspoon salt
3 large sticks celery
175 g (6 oz) mature
  Cheddar cheese
1 clove garlic, peeled
1 large egg (size 2)
6 tablespoons milk
Grated Cheddar cheese for
  sprinkling

Good with soup or a cheeseboard and best eaten on the day of making. An unusual type of bread, this recipe is quick to make because it has no yeast in it.

Pre-heat the oven to gas mark 5, 375°F (190°C). Lightly grease a baking tray or a 20-cm (8-inch) round cake tin. Place the flour in a large mixing bowl and rub in the margarine. Add a little freshly ground black pepper with the salt.

Grate the celery and cheese and crush the garlic. (If the celery is stringy, chop finely instead of grating.) Stir into the dry ingredients. Whisk together the egg and milk and beat into the flour mixture to form a soft dough.

Turn out onto a lightly floured surface and either shape quickly into a neat round about 20 cm (8 inches) in diameter and place on the baking tray, or divide the dough into 12 even-sized pieces and place into the prepared cake tin in the shape of a circle, starting from the outside. Sprinkle the dough with a little grated cheese.

Bake for about 40–45 minutes or until well risen, golden brown and hollow to sound when tapped on the base. Cool on a wire rack.

LARGE CAKES AND
SPONGE CAKES

These large cakes are suitable for different occasions – some for every day and more special ones for tea and bridge parties. In this chapter you will also find old favourites such as Cherry loaf cake and Dundee cake and also a Christmas cake which is extremely quick to decorate.

The all-in-one method has even made the preparation of large cakes a quick and easy task. Placing all of the main ingredients into the bowl to be mixed together means that there is no longer any danger of the mixture curdling, as there is when the eggs are beaten in one at a time and perhaps added too quickly. The use of self-raising flour and baking powder together also means that the threat of the cake not rising due to insufficient mixing is overcome.

For these larger cakes it is definitely worth getting out the food mixer, making the job simpler and quicker still. Take care not to overmix; only beat until the mixture is smooth, this usually only takes a couple of minutes.

CHERRY LOAF CAKE

•

175 g (6 oz) glacé cherries
225 g (8 oz) self-raising
   flour
175 g (6 oz) soft margarine
175 g (6 oz) caster sugar
Finely grated rind of 1
   lemon
50 g (2 oz) ground almonds
3 eggs

Always a favourite. Wash and dry the quartered cherries thoroughly to prevent them from sinking to the bottom of the cake.

Pre-heat the oven to gas mark 4, 350°F (180°C). Grease and base line a 900-g (2-lb) loaf tin with greased greaseproof paper.

Cut each cherry into quarters, put in a sieve and rinse under running water. Drain well then dry thoroughly on absorbent kitchen paper.

Measure all the remaining ingredients into a large bowl and beat well for 1 minute to mix thoroughly. Lightly fold in the cherries. Turn into the prepared tin and bake for about 1–1¼ hours or until well risen, golden brown and a skewer inserted into the centre comes out clean. Leave to cool in the tin for 10 minutes then turn out, remove the paper and finish cooling on a wire rack.

DUNDEE CAKE

•

Try to keep this cake for a week before eating as the flavour then improves.

Pre-heat the oven to gas mark 3, 325°F (160°C). Grease and base line a deep 20-cm (8-inch) round cake tin with greased greaseproof paper.

Measure the margarine, sugar, eggs, flour and baking powder into a bowl and mix together until well blended, smooth and glossy. Fold in the remaining ingredients, except the split almonds.

Spoon the mixture into the prepared tin and level the surface. Carefully arrange the split almonds in circles all over the top.

Bake for about 1½–1¾ hours or until the cake is firm and springy to touch and a skewer inserted into the centre comes out clean. Allow to cool in the tin for about 30 minutes before turning out onto a wire rack to cool completely.

Keep in an airtight container for 1 week before eating.

INGREDIENTS

150 g (5 oz) soft margarine
150 g (5 oz) light brown muscovado sugar
3 eggs
225 g (8 oz) plain flour
1 level teaspoon baking powder
100 g (4 oz) currants
100 g (4 oz) raisins
100 g (4 oz) sultanas
50 g (2 oz) glacé cherries, halved, rinsed and dried
50 g (2 oz) chopped mixed peel
2 tablespoons ground almonds
Grated rind of 1 orange and 1 lemon
50 g (2 oz) split blanched almonds

SWISS ROLL

—— • ——

INGREDIENTS

*4 eggs (size 2), at room
 temperature
100 g (4 oz) caster sugar
100 g (4 oz) self-raising
 flour*

FOR THE FILLING

*Caster sugar for sprinkling
About 4 tablespoons
 raspberry jam*

S wiss roll is truly quick and easy to make. You can make it from ingredients that you are bound to have in the store-cupboard; eggs, flour and sugar. Take care not to overwhisk the eggs and sugar. Whisk just until the mixture leaves a trail. Don't overbake or the sponge will crack when rolled up. This 4-egg mixture gives a good thick Swiss roll.

Pre-heat the oven to gas mark 7, 425°F (220°C). Grease and line a Swiss roll tin 33 × 23 cm (13 × 9 inches) with greased greaseproof paper.

Whisk the eggs and sugar together in a large bowl until the mixture is light and frothy and the whisk will leave a trail when lifted out. Sieve the flour and carefully fold into the mixture.

Turn the mixture into the tin and give it a gentle shake so that the mixture finds its own level, making sure that it spreads evenly into the corners. Bake for about 10 minutes or until the sponge is golden brown and begins to shrink from the edges of the tin.

While the cake is cooking, place a piece of non-stick baking parchment, a little bigger than the size of the tin, onto a work surface and sprinkle it with caster sugar. When cooked, invert the cake onto the sugared paper. Quickly loosen the paper on the bottom of the cake and peel it off. Trim the edges of the sponge with a sharp knife and make a score mark 2.5 cm (1 inch) in from the short rolling edge, being careful not to cut right through. Roll up the cake firmly with the sugared paper inside and allow to cool.

Warm the jam gently in a small pan until it is of a consistency that is easy to spread: if it is too hot the jam will soak straight into the sponge.

Carefully unroll the cooled cake. Remove the paper, spread with the jam and re-roll. Sprinkle with sugar.

LEMON SWISS ROLL

Add the finely grated rind of 1 lemon to the egg mixture. Fill with lemon curd in place of the jam.

CHOCOLATE SWISS ROLL

Replace 40 g (1 ½ oz) of self-raising flour with cocoa powder. Fill with about 2 tablespoons of strawberry jam and 300 ml (10 fl oz) whipped cream.

COFFEE SWISS ROLL

Fill the basic Swiss roll with coffee butter cream made with 75 g (3 oz) soft margarine, 225 g (8 oz) sieved icing sugar, 2 teaspoons milk and 2 teaspoons coffee essence.

ORANGE SWISS ROLL

Add the finely grated rind of an orange to the egg mixture. Fill with about 2 tablespoons orange marmalade and 225 g (8 oz) Greek yogurt.

RASPBERRY OR STRAWBERRY SWISS ROLL

Fill the basic Swiss roll with 300 ml (10 fl oz) whipped cream and sliced strawberries or whole raspberries, or both!

PINEAPPLE AND SULTANA CAKE

———— • ————

INGREDIENTS

*225 g (8 oz) can pineapple
rings or chunks in fruit
juice*
50 g (2 oz) glacé cherries
150 g (5 oz) butter, softened
*120 g (4 ½ oz) light
muscovado sugar*
2 large eggs (size 2)
*200 g (7 oz) self-raising
flour*
350 g (12 oz) sultanas

A lovely moist cake, but do make sure that you dry the pineapple very thoroughly. The cake will keep for up to a month in an airtight container in the fridge.

Pre-heat the oven to gas mark 3, 325°F (160°C). Grease and line the base and sides of a deep 20-cm (8-inch) round cake tin with greased greaseproof paper.

Drain the pineapple reserving 2 tablespoons of the juice. Dry the pineapple very thoroughly on absorbent kitchen paper then chop finely. Quarter the cherries then wash and dry thoroughly.

Measure the butter, sugar, eggs, and flour into a mixing bowl. Mix together until thoroughly blended, smooth and glossy. Fold in the pineapple, cherries and sultanas and the reserved pineapple juice. Turn into the prepared cake tin and bake for about 1 ¼–1 ½ hours or until the cake is a pale golden brown, firm to the touch and shrinking away from the sides of the tin.

Leave to cool in the tin, then remove the paper.

COFFEE AND WALNUT SPONGE CAKE

—— • ——

Coffee essence is good to use in baking. However, if you haven't any in the cupboard use 2 teaspoons of instant coffee mixed with 1 tablespoon of hot water. Use a little more in the cake mixture than in the icing.

▬▬▬

Pre-heat the oven to gas mark 3, 325°F (160°C). Grease and base line two 18-cm (7-inch) sandwich tins with greased greaseproof paper.

Measure the margarine, sugar, eggs, flour, baking powder, chopped walnuts and coffee essence into a bowl. Beat together until thoroughly blended and smooth.

Divide the mixture between the sponge sandwich tins and level the surface.

Bake for about 35–40 minutes or until well risen and the top of the cake springs back when lightly pressed with a finger. Leave to cool in the tins for a few minutes then turn out, peel off the paper and finish cooling on a wire rack.

To make the filling: beat the margarine, sieved icing sugar, milk and coffee essence in a bowl until smooth. When the cakes are completely cold sandwich together with half of the filling and use the rest for the top of the cake. Decorate with the walnut halves.

INGREDIENTS

100 g (4 oz) soft margarine
100 g (4 oz) caster sugar
2 eggs
100 g (4 oz) self-raising
  flour
1 teaspoon baking powder
50 g (2 oz) walnuts,
  chopped
1 tablespoon coffee essence
FOR THE FILLING
75 g (3 oz) soft margarine
225 g (8 oz) icing sugar,
  sieved
2 teaspoons milk
2 teaspoons coffee essence
8 walnut halves

ALMOND SPICE CAKE

———— • ————

100 g (4 oz) white almond
  paste
75 g (3 oz) flaked almonds
175 g (6 oz) soft margarine
175 g (6 oz) caster sugar
3 eggs
225 g (8 oz) self-raising
  flour
2 teaspoons baking powder
½ teaspoon ground cinnamon
¼ teaspoon ground cloves

FOR THE TOPPING
50 g (2 oz) butter
100 g (4 oz) light
  muscovado sugar
2 tablespoons double cream
25 g (1 oz) flaked almonds

To save time it makes sense to toast the almonds for the cake and the topping at the same time. Do remember to reserve 25 g (1 oz) for the top!

Pre-heat the oven to gas mark 4, 350°F (180°C). Grease and base line a deep 18-cm (7-inch) round cake tin with greased greaseproof paper.

Roll out the almond paste to an 18-cm (7-inch) circle. Leave on one side. Toast the flaked almonds for the cake and topping. Measure the margarine, sugar, eggs, flour, baking powder and spices into a bowl and beat well until thoroughly blended. Fold in 75 g (3 oz) of the toasted flaked almonds.

Spoon half of the cake mixture into the prepared cake tin and level the surface. Lightly place the circle of almond paste on top, add the remaining cake mixture and level the surface.

Bake for about 1–1¼ hours or until well risen, golden brown and the surface springs back when lightly pressed with a finger. Cool in the tin for 5 minutes before turning out onto a wire rack to cool.

For the topping: in a saucepan heat the butter, sugar and cream together until blended. Bring to the boil. Place a baking tray under the cake on the cooling rack to catch any drips, then drizzle the icing over the cake. Sprinkle with the remaining 25 g (1 oz) of toasted flaked almonds. Allow to cool for 10–15 minutes to set.

Opposite: BORROWDALE TEABREAD (*Page 22*)
Overleaf: PINEAPPLE AND SULTANA CAKE (*Page 30*)

QUICK CHRISTMAS CAKE

———— • ————

You do need to be organized to soak the fruit the night before but precious time can be saved when making the cake by using mixed dried fruit and the all-in-one mixing method. Don't worry about skinning the almonds either.

It is now also possible to buy very good almond paste and all-in-one royal icing to save you making your own. The quantity given for the almond paste is on the generous side to make covering the cake even quicker and easier.

Measure the dried fruit and prepared cherries into a bowl, add the brandy, stir to mix, cover and leave in a cool place overnight.

Pre-heat the oven to gas mark 1, 275°F (140°C). Grease and line the base and sides of a deep 20-cm (8-inch) round cake tin with a double layer of greased greaseproof paper. Measure the remaining ingredients for the cake into a large mixing bowl and beat together thoroughly until well blended and smooth.

Add the soaked fruit and any liquid and mix well. Turn into the prepared tin and bake for about 4½ hours or until the cake is well risen, firm to the touch, and a skewer inserted into the centre comes out clean. Cover the top of the cake with foil after 3 hours if it is becoming too brown.

Allow the cake to cool in the tin, then make holes with a skewer all over the top and feed it with more brandy. When completely cold, take the cake out of the tin and wrap in a double layer of greaseproof paper and foil. Feed at intervals with brandy until you need to ice the cake.

To decorate, measure the apricot jam into a pan and heat gently until boiling. Brush all over the cake. Roll the almond paste out on a surface lightly dusted with icing sugar to a thickness of about 5 mm (¼ inch) and large enough to cover the whole cake. Carefully lift the almond paste over the cake and smooth it over the top and sides with your hand. Trim the excess almond paste from the base of the cake. Place the cake on a cake board 5 cm (2 inches) larger than the cake. Make up the royal icing following the packet instructions. Cover the cake with a thick layer of the icing then 'peak' the icing with the back of a spoon to form a snow effect. Leave to set.

INGREDIENTS

900 g (2 lb) mixed dried fruit
50 g (2 oz) glacé cherries, quartered, rinsed and dried
3 tablespoons brandy
225 g (8 oz) plain flour
¼ teaspoon freshly grated nutmeg
½ teaspoon ground mixed spice
225 g (8 oz) soft margarine
225 g (8 oz) light brown muscovado sugar
4 eggs
50 g (2 oz) whole almonds, chopped
1 rounded tablespoon black treacle
Grated rind of 1 orange and 1 lemon
A little brandy to feed

TO DECORATE
3–4 tablespoons apricot jam
900 g (2 lb) almond paste
Icing sugar for dusting
Large cake board or foil-covered baking tray
450 g (1 lb) packet all-in-one royal icing

ALMOND AND CHOCOLATE CHIP CAKE

•

INGREDIENTS

225 g (8 oz) self-raising
  flour
175 g (6 oz) soft margarine
175 g (6 oz) caster sugar
3 eggs, size 2
50 g (2 oz) ground almonds
175 g (6 oz) plain chocolate
  chips
1 teaspoon vanilla essence
Flaked almonds for
  sprinkling

A lovely cake to make as a treat for the family.

Pre-heat the oven to gas mark 4, 350°F (180°C). Grease and base line a deep 18-cm (7-inch) round cake tin with greased greaseproof paper.

Measure the flour, margarine, sugar, eggs, ground almonds, chocolate chips and vanilla essence into a large bowl and beat well for about 2 minutes until thoroughly mixed.

Turn the mixture into the prepared tin and level the surface. Sprinkle the top liberally with flaked almonds. Bake in the oven for about 1-1¼ hours or until well risen and firm to the touch.

Leave the cake to cool in the tin for 10 minutes then turn out and finish cooling on a wire rack.

BISCUITS AND COOKIES

Nothing disappears faster than home made biscuits – they have a much better flavour than any shop bought ones and it is possible to make many more interesting varieties than are available in the shops.

Take care with the timing when you are baking biscuits, they are small and thin and therefore will overcook very quickly. Use the time given in the recipe as a guide, but watch the colour of the biscuits carefully as they cook.

Traditionally, the biscuit dough was always rolled out and then cut into shapes with biscuit cutters, but there are many biscuit mixtures today which can be spooned straight onto the baking tray, or simply rolled into balls and baked.

Biscuits are ideal for batch baking but don't leave them all in the tin. Freeze some to maintain their freshness.

CORNISH FAIRINGS

M A K E S

—— about 24 ——

INGREDIENTS

100 g (4 oz) plain flour
¼ teaspoon ground ginger
¼ teaspoon ground mixed
spice
¼ teaspoon ground cinnamon
½ teaspoon bicarbonate of
soda
50 g (2 oz) soft margarine
50 g (2 oz) caster sugar
2 tablespoons golden syrup

Take care not to bake these too long as they become hard and too crisp. You may well question banging the baking tray part way through cooking. This is just as the Cornish cooks have done through the ages.

———

Pre-heat the oven to gas mark 4, 350°F (180°C). Lightly grease 2 baking trays.

Sift the flour, spices and bicarbonate of soda into a bowl. Rub the margarine into the flour mixture. Mix in the sugar. Gently melt the syrup in a small pan and stir into the mixture to make a soft dough.

Roll the mixture into balls about the size of a cherry and place on the baking trays, allowing room for them to spread. Bake for 10 minutes then take the baking trays out of the oven and hit on a solid surface to make the biscuits crack and spread.

Bake for a further 5 minutes until a good even brown. Cool on a wire rack.

SHREWSBURY BISCUITS

M A K E S

—— about 24 ——

These traditional English biscuits are often confused with Easter biscuits – both may be flavoured with lemon, dried fruit or spices, with a sugary topping.

Pre-heat the oven to gas mark 4, 350°F (180°C). Lightly grease 2–3 baking trays.

Mix together the flour and sugar and rub in the fat until the mixture resembles fine breadcrumbs. Add the currants with the lemon rind and juice and sufficient egg to make a stiff dough.

Roll the biscuit mixture out thinly and cut into rounds using a 6-cm (2½-inch) fluted cutter.

Place on the baking trays and bake for about 15 minutes, or until turning golden at the edges. Lift onto a cooling rack and allow to cool.

INGREDIENTS

225 g (8 oz) self-raising flour
100 g (4 oz) caster sugar
100 g (4 oz) soft margarine
50 g (2 oz) currants
Grated rind and juice ½ lemon
1 egg, beaten

MELTING MOMENTS

MAKES

—— about 24 ——

INGREDIENTS

100 g (4 oz) soft margarine
75 g (3 oz) caster sugar
1 egg yolk
Few drops vanilla essence
150 g (5 oz) self-raising
   flour
25 g (1 oz) rolled oats
6 glacé cherries (optional)

Crushed cornflakes can be used in place of the rolled oats if you prefer. You could also place a quartered cherry on the top if they're for children.

———————

Pre-heat the oven to gas mark 5, 375°F (190°C). Lightly grease 2 baking trays.

Measure the margarine, sugar, egg yolk, vanilla essence and flour into a mixing bowl. Mix together to form a soft dough. Divide the mixture into about 24 portions.

Form each piece into a ball and roll in the oats to cover. Flatten each ball slightly and top each with a quartered glacé cherry if desired.

Place well apart on the baking trays and bake for about 15–20 minutes or until golden. Allow to cool slightly on the baking trays for a few moments before lifting onto a wire rack to cool.

FAST FLAPJACKS

M A K E S

—— 12 ——

While there is nothing particularly fast about this flap-jack recipe, flapjacks are very quick to make. The results will be crunchy, traditional and delicious.

———

Pre-heat the oven to gas mark 3, 325°F (160°C). Lightly grease a shallow 18-cm (7-inch) square tin.

Melt the margarine in a pan with the sugar and syrup and then stir in the oats. Mix well and then turn into the prepared tin and press flat with a palette knife or the back of a spoon.

Bake for about 35 minutes or until pale golden brown. Remove from the oven and then leave to cool for 10 minutes. Mark into 12 squares and leave to finish cooling in the tin.

INGREDIENTS

100 g (4 oz) margarine
100 g (4 oz) demerara sugar
1 level tablespoon golden
  syrup
150 g (5 oz) rolled oats

CHOCOLATE CHIP COOKIES

M A K E S
—— about 24 ——

75 g (3 oz) soft margarine
100 g (4 oz) caster sugar
1 egg
175 g (6 oz) self-raising
  flour
50 g (2 oz) plain chocolate
  chips

Roughly chop plain chocolate if you don't have any chocolate chips.

Pre-heat the oven to gas mark 4, 350°F (180°C). Lightly grease 2 baking trays.

Place all of the ingredients into a medium bowl and mix thoroughly until a smooth dough is formed. Place small spoonfuls of the mixture well apart on the baking trays and flatten slightly using the back of a spoon. Bake for about 15 minutes or until golden brown and just firm to the touch.

Cool on a wire rack and store in an airtight container.

THE VERY BEST SHORTBREAD

M A K E S

—— 8 wedges ——

For a really good shortbread it is essential to use butter not margarine. Cornflour or ground rice can replace the semolina. You can make a larger thinner circle if you like thin shortbread, but remember the cooking time will be shorter if you do this.

INGREDIENTS

100 g (4 oz) plain flour
50 g 2 oz semolina
100 g (4 oz) butter
50 g (2 oz) caster sugar
25 g (1 oz) flaked almonds
(optional)
Caster sugar for dusting

Lightly grease a baking tray.

Mix the flour with the semolina in a bowl or food processor. Add the butter and sugar and rub together with the finger tips, or process in the food processor, until the mixture is just beginning to bind together. Knead lightly until the mixture forms a smooth dough.

Place the dough onto the greased baking tray and roll out to an 18-cm (7-inch) circle. Crimp the edges to decorate and prick all over with a fork. Mark into 8 wedges, sprinkle over the flaked almonds, if using, and chill until firm. Meanwhile pre-heat the oven to gas mark 3, 325°F (160°C).

Bake for about 35 minutes or until a very pale golden brown. Re-mark the sections, dust with the caster sugar and leave to cool on the baking tray for about 5 minutes. Carefully lift off with a palette knife and finish cooling on a wire rack.

Alternatively, press the dough out into a greased 18-cm (7-inch) sandwich tin, bake as before and then mark into 8 wedges. Leave to cool in the tin and sprinkle with caster sugar.

RICH CHEESY BISCUITS

M A K E S

—— about 32 ——

INGREDIENTS

175 g (6 oz) plain flour
¾ teaspoon salt
¾ teaspoon dry mustard
   powder
75 g (3 oz) butter
175 g (6 oz) mature
   Cheddar cheese, grated
2 small eggs (size 4)
Sesame or poppy seeds for
   sprinkling

Good to go with drinks. If these are made ahead they are best just heated through in the oven before serving.

Pre-heat the oven to gas mark 6, 400°F (200°C). Lightly grease 3 baking trays.

Sift the flour, salt and mustard powder into a bowl and rub in the butter until the mixture resembles fine breadcrumbs. Stir in the grated cheese.

Beat the eggs, then stir just enough egg into the flour mixture to form a soft dough. (There should be a little left over for glazing.) Wrap the dough in cling film and chill for about 15 minutes.

Roll the dough out to a thickness of about 5 mm (¼ inch) and cut into 5-cm (2-inch) rounds or triangles. Place on the baking trays and brush with the remaining beaten egg. Sprinkle lightly with sesame or poppy seeds. Re-roll the trimmings once only.

Bake for about 10–15 minutes or until crisp and golden. Cool on a wire rack.

FAMILY CAKES

These are mainly family favourites. Although there are some 90 recipes in this book, I know that many people will go for the classic Victoria sandwich which is now so fast to make with the new soft margarines.

Family cakes are 'proper' cakes – not dainty, fancy or individual but cakes for the family to really tuck into.

Take a little time to master the cakes in this chapter, you will then be able to rely on these favourites to please everybody whether for a lunchbox or Sunday tea.

ALL-IN-ONE VICTORIA SANDWICH CAKE

•

175 g (6 oz) soft margarine
175 g (6 oz) caster sugar
3 eggs
175 g (6 oz) self-raising
  flour
1 ½ teaspoons baking powder
FOR THE FILLING
  AND TOPPING
About 4 tablespoons
  strawberry or *raspberry*
  jam
Caster sugar for dusting

This 3-egg mixture makes a good deep sandwich cake.

Pre-heat the oven to gas mark 4, 350°F (180°C). Grease and base line two 18-cm (7-inch) sandwich cake tins with greased greaseproof paper.

Measure the margarine, sugar, eggs, flour and baking powder into a large bowl and beat well until thoroughly blended. Divide the mixture between the 2 tins and level out evenly.

Bake for about 25 minutes, or until well risen, and the tops of the cakes spring back when lightly pressed with a finger. Leave to cool in the tins for a few moments then turn out, peel off the paper and finish cooling on a wire rack.

When completely cold, sandwich the 2 cakes together with the jam. Sprinkle with caster sugar to serve.

ORANGE OR LEMON CAKE

Add the finely grated rind of 1 orange or 1 lemon to the cake mixture. Sandwich together with lemon curd or orange marmalade. Sprinkle with caster sugar to serve.

CHOCOLATE CAKE

Blend 2 tablespoons sieved cocoa with 3 tablespoons boiling water in a mixing bowl. Cool, then add the remaining ingredients and continue as above. (No need to decrease the amount of flour in the recipe.) Sandwich together and cover the top with white butter cream: blend together 50 g (2 oz) soft margarine, 175 g (6 oz) sieved icing sugar and 1 tablespoon milk. Decorate with coarsely grated chocolate.

COFFEE CAKE

Dissolve 2 heaped teaspoons of instant coffee in the beaten eggs before adding to the bowl. Sandwich the cakes together with coffee butter cream: add 1 tablespoon coffee essence to the white butter cream in the chocolate cake recipe above.

CUT AND COME AGAIN CAKE

———— • ————

This is a traditional name for a cake that is so delicious that 'you'll come again' and have another piece. Good for a hungry family, this is not a rich cake so it is best eaten as fresh as possible.

INGREDIENTS

350 g (12 oz) self-raising flour
1 teaspoon mixed spice
175 g (6 oz) soft margarine
175 g (6 oz) caster sugar
3 eggs
175 g (6 oz) currants
100 g (4 oz) sultanas
100 g (4 oz) raisins
3 tablespoons milk

Pre-heat the oven to gas mark 4, 350°F (180°C). Grease and base line a deep 20-cm (8-inch) round cake tin with greased greaseproof paper.

Measure all the ingredients into a large bowl and beat well until thoroughly mixed. Turn into the prepared tin and level the surface evenly.

Bake for about 1 ¼ – 1 ½ hours or until a skewer inserted into the centre of the cake comes out clean. Leave to cool in the tin for about 10 minutes, then turn out, peel off the paper and finish cooling on a wire rack.

STICKY GINGER AND ORANGE CAKE

•

100 g (4 oz) golden syrup
100 g (4 oz) black treacle
100 g (4 oz) soft margarine
100 g (4 oz) caster sugar
Grated rind of 1 orange
1 egg, beaten
275 g (10 oz) plain flour
1 ½ teaspoons bicarbonate of soda
1 teaspoon ground cinnamon
1 teaspoon ground ginger

FOR THE ICING
100 g (4 oz) icing sugar
Juice of 1 orange

If possible store the cake for 2 days wrapped in greaseproof paper and foil before icing. This allows the cake to mature and become moist and sticky.

Pre-heat the oven to gas mark 4, 350°F (180°C). Grease and line a deep 23-cm (9-inch) round cake tin with greased greaseproof paper.

Put the golden syrup and black treacle into a pan with 250 ml (8 fl oz) water and bring to the boil.

Meanwhile, place the remaining ingredients into a mixing bowl and beat well until thoroughly blended. Add the syrup and treacle mixture, beating well until smooth.

Pour the mixture into the prepared tin and bake for about 50 minutes or until a skewer inserted into the centre comes out clean.

Cool in the tin for 10 minutes before turning out onto a wire rack to cool completely.

To make the icing: sift the icing sugar into a bowl and add enough orange juice to make a smooth, fairly thick mixture. Stand the wire rack over a baking tray to catch the drips, then spoon the icing over the top of the cake and leave to set for about 1 hour.

*W*I MINCEMEAT LOAF CAKES

———— • ————

To make one loaf cake you can easily halve the recipe, but it seems sensible when the oven is on to make full use of the heat and make two. The second cake will freeze or store very well.

Why WI? I often see my recipe for sale on Women's Institute market stalls, where the cakes are always of a very professional standard.

——————

Pre-heat the oven to gas mark 3, 325°F (160°C). Grease and base line two 450-g (1-lb) loaf tins with greased greaseproof paper.

Measure all the ingredients into a large bowl and mix well until evenly blended. Turn into the prepared tins and level out the surface.

Bake for about 1 ¼ hours, or until well risen, golden brown and a skewer inserted into the centre comes out clean.

Allow to cool for a few minutes in the tins, then turn out, peel off the paper and finish cooling on a wire rack.

INGREDIENTS

2 eggs
150 g (5 oz) caster sugar
150 g (5 oz) soft margarine
225 g (8 oz) self-raising
   flour
350 g (12 oz) mincemeat
225 g (8 oz) currants

BANANA LOAF CAKE

1 teaspoon bicarbonate of
  soda
2 tablespoons boiling milk
100 g (4 oz) soft margarine
175 g (6 oz) caster sugar
2 eggs, beaten
2 ripe bananas, mashed
225 g (8 oz) plain flour
1 teaspoon baking powder

This proved very popular in one of my very early TV programmes. It is such a good way of using up over-ripe bananas.

Pre-heat the oven to gas mark 4, 350°F (180°C). Lightly grease and base line a 900-g (2-lb) loaf tin with greased greaseproof paper.

Stir the bicarbonate of soda into the milk in a large bowl. Cool slightly. Measure all of the remaining ingredients into the bowl and beat well until thoroughly blended.

Turn the cake mixture into the prepared tin and bake for about 1 hour or until well risen, golden brown and springy to the touch.

Turn out and leave to cool on a wire rack. Serve sliced by itself or spread with butter.

'BOOZY' FRUIT CAKE

——— • ———

Excellent if short of time, this cake is quick to make and needs no maturing.

Pre-heat the oven to gas mark 2, 300°F (150°C). Grease a deep 20-cm (8-inch) round cake tin and line the base and sides with a double layer of greased greaseproof paper.

Roughly chop the dates. Measure the margarine, syrup, milk, fruit, including the chopped dates, mixed peel and nuts into a pan and gently heat, stirring occasionally, until the fat has melted. Simmer very gently for 5 minutes. Allow to cool slightly.

Sift the flour, spice and bicarbonate of soda into a bowl, add the syrup mixture and the eggs, and beat together until thoroughly combined.

Pour into the prepared tin and bake for 1½–1¾ hours or until firm to the touch and a skewer inserted into the centre comes out clean.

Leave to cool in the tin for 10 minutes. To feed, skewer the cake at intervals and spoon over the brandy.

INGREDIENTS

100 g (4 oz) dried stoned dates
150 g (5 oz) soft margarine
175 g (6 oz) golden syrup
175 ml (6 fl oz) milk
150 g (5 oz) sultanas
150 g (5 oz) raisins
50 g (2 oz) currants
50 g (2 oz) chopped mixed peel
100 g (4 oz) walnut pieces
225 g (8 oz) plain flour
2 teaspoons ground mixed spice
½ teaspoon bicarbonate of soda
2 eggs
A little brandy to feed

OLD-FASHIONED SEED CAKE

———— • ————

225 g (8 oz) self-raising
  flour
1 teaspoon baking powder
150 g (5 oz) butter, softened
150 g (5 oz) caster sugar
2 eggs
2 tablespoons milk
50 g (2 oz) chopped mixed
  peel
2 teaspoons caraway seeds

You either love or loathe seed cake – this one has a good buttery flavour and tastes wonderful. The chopped mixed peel is optional in this recipe but it does add a lovely flavour and texture to the cake.

————

Pre-heat the oven to gas mark 4, 350°F (180°C). Grease and base line a deep 18-cm (7-inch) round cake tin with greased greaseproof paper.

Measure all the ingredients except the mixed peel and caraway seeds into a large bowl. Beat well for about 1 minute until thoroughly blended. Carefully fold in the mixed peel and caraway seeds, reserving a few seeds to sprinkle over the cake.

Turn the mixture into the prepared tin and sprinkle over the reserved seeds. Bake for about 1 hour or until well risen, golden brown and a skewer inserted into the centre comes out clean.

Allow to cool in the tin for 10 minutes before turning out and cooling on a wire rack.

CHOCOLATE CAKES

Rich and irresistible, chocolate can be used to bake and to decorate cakes in many different ways.

Cocoa powder undoubtedly gives the most inexpensive, strongest and best flavour in baking, don't try to substitute drinking chocolate.

Plain chocolate, such as Bournville, has a rich strong flavour where real chocolate is needed. The flavour of the sweeter milk chocolate tends to be lost in baking but it is good for decoration. Use chocolate-flavoured cake covering for quick decorations.

To melt chocolate successfully, break it up into a bowl and place this over a pan of gently simmering water. Allow the chocolate to melt *slowly*, occasionally stirring, until the chocolate is smooth and glossy. Take care not to allow steam or water into the chocolate or it will become stiff and granular.

DATE AND CHOCOLATE LOAF

•

INGREDIENTS

*150 g (5 oz) dried stoned
dates*
150 g (5 oz) plain chocolate
40 g (1 ½ oz) soft margarine
150 g (5 oz) Brazil nuts
225 g (8 oz) plain flour
40 g (1 ½ oz) caster sugar
1 teaspoon baking powder
*1 teaspoon bicarbonate of
soda*
1 egg
150 ml (5 fl oz) milk
Demerara sugar for dusting

A moist, rich loaf which needs no buttering.

Pre-heat the oven to gas mark 4, 350°F (180°C). Grease and base line a 900-g (2-lb) loaf tin with greased greaseproof paper.

Roughly chop the dates and place in a small bowl. Pour over 150 ml (5 fl oz) boiling water and leave to soak for about 30 minutes.

Break up the chocolate and melt with the margarine in a small bowl, set over a pan of simmering water. Roughly chop the Brazil nuts, reserve about 2 tablespoons for decoration.

In a bowl mix together the flour, caster sugar, baking powder and bicarbonate of soda.

Mix together the egg and milk and beat this into the dry ingredients adding the nuts, dates and their soaking liquid, and the chocolate mixture.

Spoon into the prepared tin, level the surface and sprinkle over the reserved nuts with the demerara sugar. Bake for about 1 hour 10 minutes or until a skewer inserted into the centre comes out clean. Cover loosely with foil towards the end of cooking time if the cake is becoming too brown.

Cool in the tin for 10 minutes before turning out onto a wire rack to cool.

CHOCOLATE CHIP BROWNIES

M A K E S

—— about 20 ——

Very wicked – to be eaten in small squares as suggested. Expect the centre to dip a little like a gingerbread.

INGREDIENTS

175 g (6 oz) unsalted butter
175 g (6 oz) plain chocolate
120 g (4 ½ oz) self-raising flour
350 g (12 oz) light muscovado sugar
4 eggs, lightly beaten
75 g (3 oz) milk chocolate chips

Pre-heat the oven to gas mark 4, 350°F (180°C). Grease and base line a 30 × 23 cm (12 × 9 inch) roasting tin with greased greaseproof paper.

Cut the butter up into small pieces, break up the chocolate and gently melt the two together in a bowl placed over a pan of hot water.

Mix together the flour, sugar and lightly beaten eggs. Add the slightly cooled chocolate mixture and stir well until thoroughly blended.

Add the chocolate chips and pour into the prepared tin. Bake for about 45–50 minutes or until just firm to the touch. Cool in the tin and cut into squares to serve.

BLACK FOREST CAKE

SERVES

—— 10–12 ——

4 eggs
100 g (4 oz) caster sugar
75 g (3 oz) self-raising flour,
  sieved
25 g (1 oz) cocoa, sieved
FOR THE FILLING AND
  TOPPING
2 × 425 g (15 oz) cans
  stoned black cherries
2 tablespoons cornflour
4 tablespoons kirsch
450 ml (15 fl oz) whipping
  cream, whipped
Grated chocolate to decorate

This classic cake is often thought of as a party dessert which is complicated to decorate. My version shows that with a few variations the decoration can be much quicker and simpler but equally effective.

A very moist cake, the juices soak into the sponge giving an almost trifly consistency.

If you are assembling this cake on the day, don't bother to thicken the juices.

Pre-heat the oven to gas mark 4, 350°F (180°C). Grease and base line a deep 23-cm (9-inch) round cake tin with greased greaseproof paper.

Break the eggs into a mixing bowl, add the sugar and whisk until the mixture is pale and thick enough to leave a trail when lifted out of the bowl.

Carefully fold in the sieved flour and cocoa. Turn the mixture into the prepared tin.

Bake for about 40–45 minutes until the sponge is well risen and beginning to shrink away from the sides of the tin. Turn out onto a wire rack to cool.

Drain the cans of cherries, reserving the juice. Keep a few whole cherries for the top and stone the remainder. Place the cornflour in a small saucepan and gradually stir in the cherry juice. Bring slowly to the boil, stirring until thickened, simmer for 2 minutes, then remove from the heat and cool. Add the kirsch and the stoned cherries to the sauce.

Cut the sponge into 3 layers with a long sharp knife. Sandwich the layers together with most of the whipped cream and all of the cherry mixture.

Decorate the top with the remaining cream, reserved cherries and grated chocolate (or chocolate curls if you prefer).

CHOCOLATE ROULADE

S E R V E S

—— 6–8 ——

A lways a favourite, this is a luxury one with brandy! Don't worry that the sponge cracks as it is rolled – it is meant to and is part of its charm.

———

Pre-heat the oven to gas mark 4, 350°F (180°C). Grease and line a 33 × 23 cm (13 × 9 inch) Swiss roll tin with greased greaseproof paper.

Break the chocolate into small pieces and place in a bowl with the brandy. Set the bowl over a pan of simmering water and allow the chocolate to melt gently.

Measure the egg yolks and sugar into a large bowl and whisk until light and creamy. Carefully stir in the melted chocolate until evenly blended.

Whisk the egg whites in another bowl until stiff but not dry and fold gently into the chocolate mixture. Turn into the prepared tin and gently ease the mixture into the corners. Bake for about 20 minutes until firm to the touch.

Remove from the oven and, while still hot, place a dry tea towel gently down on top of the cake. On top of this put another tea towel that has been soaked with cold water and well rung out. Leave in a cool place overnight.

To finish the roulade, remove the tea towels and invert the cake onto a piece of greaseproof paper which has been liberally sprinkled with icing sugar. Remove the greaseproof paper lining and spread the cake with the whipped cream. Roll up the roulade from the long edge using the paper to help and dust with more icing sugar to decorate.

INGREDIENTS

175 g (6 oz) plain chocolate
3 tablespoons brandy
6 eggs (size 2), separated
175 g (6 oz) caster sugar
TO FINISH
Icing sugar for dusting
300 ml (10 fl oz) double
   cream, whipped

DOUBLE CHOCOLATE COOKIES

M A K E S

—— about 36 ——

D ead easy to make, these are wonderful cookies. Expect an irregular shape. They are very soft when they come out of the oven but will harden up considerably on cooling.

200-g (7-oz) bar plain chocolate
50 g (2 oz) margarine
400-g (14-oz) can condensed milk
225 g (8 oz) self-raising flour
65-g (2 ½-oz) packet milk or white chocolate buttons

Pre–heat the oven to gas mark 4, 350°F (180°C). Lightly grease 3 baking trays.

Break up the chocolate and place it with the margarine into a bowl. Melt gently over a pan of simmering water. Stir in the condensed milk then take off the heat and cool. Mix in the flour and the chocolate buttons and chill the mixture until firm enough to handle.

Place large teaspoonfuls of the mixture onto the baking trays and bake for about 15 minutes. They will still look soft and will glisten, but don't overcook them as they soon become very hard.

Carefully remove the cookies with a palette knife and cool on a wire rack.

AMERICAN CHOCOLATE MUFFINS

M A K E S

—— about 12 ——

T hese are best served warm, straight from the oven. They also freeze well and when thawed can be warmed through in a hot oven to serve.

Deep muffin tins make all the difference to the finished shape of these moreish cakes. They do need greasing as the mixture will rise above the paper cases giving the traditional muffin shape.

Use deep mince pie tins if you don't have proper muffin tins to make these.

Pre-heat the oven to gas mark 7, 425°F (220°C). Grease 12 deep muffin tins, if using, and place a paper case in each. (Ordinary bun tins do not need to be greased as the paper cases come up to the top of these tins.)

Break the chocolate into small pieces, place in a bowl and melt over a pan of simmering water. Roughly chop the walnut pieces. Remove the chocolate from the heat and beat in the nuts with the remaining ingredients.

Spoon the mixture into the paper cases and bake for about 15–20 minutes, or until well risen and firm to the touch. Serve warm.

INGREDIENTS

100 g (4 oz) plain chocolate
100 g (4 oz) walnut pieces
225 g (8 oz) self-raising
 flour
1 teaspoon baking powder
25 g (1 oz) cocoa, sieved
175 g (6 oz) caster sugar
200 ml (7 fl oz) milk
4 tablespoons sunflower oil
1 large egg (size 1)

CHOCOLATE FUDGE CAKE

•

INGREDIENTS

2 rounded tablespoons cocoa
4 tablespoons hot water
225 g (8 oz) soft margarine
225 g (8 oz) caster sugar
4 large eggs (size 2)
225 g (8 oz) self-raising
  flour
2 teaspoons baking powder

FOR THE ICING
50 g (2 oz) margarine
25 g (1 oz) cocoa, sieved
About 3 tablespoons milk
225 g (8 oz) icing sugar,
  sieved

TO FINISH
A little warmed apricot jam
  (optional)
Chocolate flake or grated
  chocolate

To make this cake even more special, do take time to heat a little apricot jam to brush over the cooled cake before icing. This will also keep the cake moist.

The icing is simple to make; avoid getting it too hot as it loses its shine. If you make it ahead and it goes hard, just gently re-heat until runny.

Pre-heat the oven to gas mark 4, 350°F (180°C). Grease and base line two 20-cm (8-inch) sandwich cake tins with greased greaseproof paper.

To make the cake: blend the cocoa with the hot water in a large bowl and leave to cool. Add the remaining cake ingredients to the bowl and beat thoroughly for 1–2 minutes. Divide between the tins and bake for about 35–40 minutes or until the cake has shrunk slightly from the sides of the tins and the cake springs back when pressed lightly with a finger. Turn out, remove the paper and leave to cool on a wire rack.

To make the icing: melt the margarine in a small pan, add the cocoa and cook for 1 minute. Remove from the heat and stir in the milk and icing sugar. Beat well until smooth. Cool until of a spreading consistency.

Spread a little warmed apricot jam on the underneath side of one of the cakes and top with half of the fudge icing. Place the remaining cake on top, spread with apricot jam as before and top with the remaining fudge icing, warmed if necessary to help you spread it. Decorate with chocolate flake or grated chocolate.

DEVIL'S FOOD CAKE

— • —

This lovely moist chocolate cake is wonderfully easy to make and keeps very well too. The classic topping is quick American frosting. It's very easy to make by simply measuring the ingredients into a bowl and whisking until thick over a pan of hot water. The mixture will become light and frothy, and when swirled over the cake will become set upon cooling.

Pre-heat the oven to gas mark 3, 325°F (160°C). Grease and base line two 20-cm (8-inch) sandwich cake tins with greased greaseproof paper.

Break the eggs into a large mixing bowl. Add the remaining ingredients for the cake and beat well for about 2 minutes, until thoroughly mixed. Divide between the two tins. Bake for about 30–35 minutes until the cakes spring back when lightly pressed with a finger and are shrinking away slightly from the sides of the tin. Leave for a few moments in the tin then turn out, peel off the paper and finish cooling on a wire rack.

For the filling and topping: place all ingredients in a bowl over a pan of hot water and whisk for 10–12 minutes until thick. Use immediately, both to fill the cake and swirling it on the top and sides of the cake with a palette knife.

INGREDIENTS

2 eggs
150 ml (5 fl oz) sunflower
  oil
150 ml (5 fl oz) milk
2 tablespoons golden syrup
150 g (5 oz) caster sugar
185 g (6 ½ oz) self-raising
  flour
25 g (1 oz) cocoa, sieved
1 teaspoon baking powder
1 teaspoon bicarbonate of
  soda

FOR THE TOPPING AND
  FILLING
175 g (6 oz) caster sugar
1 egg white
2 tablespoons hot water
Pinch of cream of tartar

CHOCOLATE ECLAIRS

MAKES

—— about 12 ——

FOR THE CHOUX PASTRY
*50 g (2 oz) margarine or
butter*
150 ml (5 fl oz) water
*65 g (2 ½ oz) plain flour,
sieved*
2 eggs, beaten

FOR THE FILLING
*300 ml (10 fl oz) whipping
cream, whipped*

FOR THE ICING
*50 g (2 oz) plain chocolate,
broken into pieces*
2 tablespoons water
15 g (½ oz) butter
*75 g (3 oz) icing sugar,
sieved*

Eclairs are always delicious for afternoon tea or as a dessert. The eclairs must be really well cooked, though, until firm and a good straw colour.

Pre-heat the oven to gas mark 7, 425°F, (220°C). Lightly grease two baking trays.

To make the pastry, measure the margarine and water into a small pan. Allow the fat to melt and then bring slowly to the boil. Remove the pan from the heat, add the flour all at once, and beat until the mixture forms a soft ball. Allow to cool slightly, then gradually beat in the eggs, beating well between each addition to give a smooth shiny paste.

Spoon the mixture into a piping bag fitted with a 1 cm (½-inch) plain nozzle and pipe into about 12 eclair shapes, about 13–15 cm (5–6 inches) long, leaving room for them to spread. Bake in the pre-heated oven for about 10 minutes, then reduce the heat to gas mark 5, 375°F (190°C) and cook for a further 20 minutes until well-risen and a deep golden brown. Remove from the oven and split one side of the eclair to allow the steam to escape. Cool on a wire rack.

Fill each eclair with a little of the whipped cream, using a piping bag with a plain nozzle.

For the icing, melt the chocolate slowly in a bowl with the water and butter over a pan of gently simmering water. Remove from the heat and beat in the sugar until smooth. Dip each eclair into the icing to coat the top, then leave to set.

LITTLE CAKES AND SCONES

Apart from looking attractive, the advantage of small cakes is that they are very quick to make and of course take less time to cook in the oven. They are perfect for children and for lunchboxes and picnics. Scones, being quick to cook, are ideal if friends unexpectedly arrive on the doorstep as they can be made and baked in minutes.

Little cakes and scones are also ideal to freeze. Pack into rigid plastic boxes or polythene bags. You can easily then take out just the number you require leaving the remainder in the freezer.

If scones have been frozen, they are best refreshed in the oven before serving. Scones left in the tin for a few days are best, and quite delicious, toasted.

CRUSTY LEMON BUNS

M A K E S

—— about 18 ——

T hese are best on the day that they are made and are good
for a picnic or lunchbox.

INGREDIENTS

100 g (4 oz) soft margarine
100 g (4 oz) caster sugar
2 eggs
100 g (4 oz) self-raising
  flour
1 teaspoon baking powder
Grated rind of 1 lemon

FOR THE SYRUP

100 g (4 oz) granulated
  sugar
Juice of 1 large lemon,
  strained

Pre-heat the oven to gas mark 6, 400°F, (200°C). Place 18
paper cake cases in bun tins.

Measure the margarine, sugar, eggs, flour, baking powder
and the grated lemon rind into a bowl. Beat well until
smooth. Divide the mixture between the paper cake cases and
bake for about 15 minutes or until well risen, golden and
springy to the touch.

Meanwhile make the syrup. Measure the sugar and strained
lemon juice into a cup or small bowl and mix together. Once
the cakes are cooked and whilst warm, place on a wire rack
positioned over a baking tray to catch the drips. Spoon over
the syrup and leave for about 30 minutes to allow the syrup to
soak in.

SWISS CAKES

MAKES
—— about 20 ——

S hort and crumbly, these smart little cakes are made by piping a creamed mixture into paper cases. Use butter for the better flavour it gives.

———

Pre-heat the oven to gas mark 4, 350°F (180°C). Place paper cake cases into about 20 bun tins.

Measure the flour, butter, icing sugar and cornflour into a food processor and blend until the mixture comes together to form a dough. Or, mix the ingredients together by hand, working the mixture until a dough is formed.

Spoon the mixture into a large piping bag fitted with a large star nozzle. Pipe a circle of the mixture into the base of each paper case until all of the mixture is used up. Bake the cakes for about 20 minutes or until golden brown. Leave to cool in the paper cases then put a small amount of jam into the centre of each cake. Dust lightly with sieved icing sugar.

INGREDIENTS

200 g (7 oz) self-raising flour
225 g (8 oz) butter, softened
75 g (3 oz) icing sugar, sieved
50 g (2 oz) cornflour
TO FINISH
A little red jam
Icing sugar for dusting

MINI ROCK CAKES

M A K E S

—— about 24 ——

225 g (8 oz) self-raising
   flour
1 teaspoon baking powder
100 g (4 oz) soft margarine
50 g (2 oz) granulated sugar
100 g (4 oz) mixed dried
   fruit
1 egg
About 1 tablespoon milk
Demerara sugar for dusting

Quick and inexpensive to make, these are best eaten on the day of making.

Pre-heat the oven to gas mark 6, 400°F (200°C). Grease 2 baking trays.

Measure the flour and baking powder into a large bowl, add the margarine and rub it in with the fingertips until the mixture resembles fine breadcrumbs. Stir in the sugar and fruit. Add the egg and milk and blend to a stiff mixture, if dry add a little more milk.

Using 2 teaspoons, shape the mixture into about 24 rough mounds on the baking trays, sprinkle with the demerara sugar and then bake for about 10 minutes or until a pale golden brown at the edges. Cool on a wire rack.

Opposite: CHOCOLATE CHIP COOKIES (*Page 42*),
THE VERY BEST SHORTBREAD (*Page 43*) and
CRACKERJACKS (*Page 129*)
Overleaf: TIRAMISU (*Page 77*) and
A SELECTION OF TRAYBAKES (*Pages 93–102*)

SCOTCH PANCAKES

M A K E S

—— about 18 ——

O therwise known as drop scones, these are very quick to make if unexpected guests drop in for tea. Aga owners can make them on the simmering plate.

INGREDIENTS

100 g (4 oz) self-raising brown or *white flour*
25 g (1 oz) caster sugar
1 egg
150 ml (5 fl oz) milk

FOR THE TOPPING
Golden syrup or blackcurrant jam

Prepare a griddle or heavy-based (non-stick) frying-pan by heating and lightly greasing it with oil or white vegetable fat.

Put the flour and sugar into a bowl, make a well in the centre and then add the egg and half of the milk and beat to a smooth thick batter. If using brown self-raising flour you may have to add a little more milk. Beat in enough of the remaining milk to make the batter the consistency of thick cream.

Drop the mixture in spoonfuls onto the hot griddle or frying-pan, spacing the mixture well apart. When the bubbles rise to the surface, turn the scones over with a palette knife and then cook them on the other side for a further 30 seconds to 1 minute until they are golden brown. Lift off onto a wire rack and cover them with a clean tea towel to keep them soft.

Continue cooking until all the batter has been used then serve warm with butter and golden syrup or blackcurrant jam.

Opposite: FILO APPLE STRUDELS (*Page 74*)

WELSH CAKES

MAKES
—— 12-14 ——

*225 g (8 oz) self-raising
  flour*
100 g (4 oz) margarine
75 g (3 oz) caster sugar
75 g (3 oz) currants
*½ teaspoon ground mixed
  spice*
1 egg
1–2 tablespoons milk
Sieved icing sugar for dusting

These lovely traditional cakes are very cheap to make, and you don't even need to turn on the oven. Aga owners can make these directly on the simmering plate.

Prepare a griddle or heavy-based (non-stick) frying-pan by heating and lightly greasing it with a little oil or white vegetable fat.

Measure the flour into a bowl and rub in the margarine until the mixture resembles fine breadcrumbs. Add the sugar, currants and spice. Beat the egg with the milk then add this to the mixture to form a firm dough.

Roll out the dough on a lightly floured work surface to a thickness of 5 mm (¼ inch) and cut into rounds with a 7.5-cm (3-inch) round cutter.

Cook the Welsh cakes on the griddle or frying-pan on a low heat for about 3 minutes on each side until golden brown. (Be careful not to cook the cakes too fast otherwise the centres will not be fully cooked through.)

Cool on a wire rack then dust with sieved icing sugar. These are best eaten on the day of making.

SPECIAL FRUIT SCONES

M A K E S
—— about 14 ——

Making good scones is so easy if the mixture is not too dry and the dough is not overhandled. Wrap the scones in a clean tea towel after baking to keep them moist.

INGREDIENTS

225 g (8 oz) self-raising
* flour*
1 teaspoon baking powder
50 g (2 oz) soft margarine
25 g (1 oz) caster sugar
50 g (2 oz) mixed dried fruit
1 egg
A little milk

Pre-heat the oven to gas mark 7, 425°F (220°C). Lightly grease 2 baking trays.

Measure the flour and baking powder into a bowl, add the margarine and rub in with the fingertips until the mixture resembles fine breadcrumbs. Stir in the sugar and the mixed dried fruit.

Break the egg into a measuring jug, then make up to 150 ml (5 fl oz) with milk. Stir the egg and milk into the flour and mix to a soft, but not sticky, dough. Turn out onto a lightly floured work surface, knead lightly and then roll out to a 1-cm (½-inch) thickness.

Cut into rounds with a fluted 5-cm (2-inch) cutter and place them on the baking trays. Brush the tops with a little milk and bake for about 10 minutes or until they are a pale golden brown. Lift scones onto a wire rack to cool. Eat as fresh as possible.

FILO APPLE STRUDELS

M A K E S

—— 8 ——

FOR THE FILLING

*350 g (12 oz) (prepared)
peeled, cored and roughly
chopped cooking apples*

Juice of ½ lemon

75 g (3 oz) demerara sugar

*25 g (1 oz) fresh brown
breadcrumbs*

50 g (2 oz) sultanas

1 teaspoon ground cinnamon

*8 sheets of filo pastry,
18 × 33 cm (7 × 13
inches)*

100 g (4 oz) butter, melted

FOR THE TOPPING

2 tablespoons caster sugar

2 tablespoons water

Icing sugar for dusting

Try to find the shorter packets of filo pastry as then you won't need to trim the pastry to size. Any filo not used will store in the fridge for 2 days, or wrap it carefully and put back into the freezer straightaway and use within 1 month.

Pre-heat the oven to gas mark 6, 400°F (200°C). Lightly grease 2 baking trays.

First prepare the filling: mix together the apple, lemon juice, sugar, breadcrumbs, sultanas and cinnamon in a bowl.

Unfold 1 sheet of filo pastry and brush liberally with melted butter. Spoon one-eighth of the apple mixture to cover the middle third of the longest edge of the pastry, leaving a small border. Fold in this border, then bring the two short sides over the apple to cover it. Roll the filled pastry over and over to form a neat strudel. Place on the baking sheet then repeat the process with the remaining pastry sheets and apple mixture.

Brush the strudels with the melted butter then bake for about 15–20 minutes or until golden brown and crisp.

Meanwhile, blend the caster sugar and water together in a small pan and heat gently until all the sugar has dissolved. Spoon the syrup over the warm strudels and dust with icing sugar to serve.

CAKES FOR DESSERT

If a cake can double up as dessert then so much the better!
Always serve these with a fork as most of them are soft and squidgy to eat.

The great bonus of these recipes is that they all freeze well. Open freeze until solid and then carefully cover. If the cake is likely to be brittle, such as a meringue, slip it into a rigid plastic box to protect it. Allow plenty of time for the cakes to thaw – usually about 8 hours at cool room temperature, the exception being the Baked Alaska which only needs to be thawed for ½-hour before baking.

Tiramisu freezes beautifully, a particular bonus if you wish to serve it for a dinner party, leaving you free on the day to concentrate on the other courses.

If you are making the Raspberry Meringue Roulade specifically for freezing and are using frozen raspberries, don't bother to thaw them first. Use them in the filling in their frozen state, freeze the whole cake and then thaw when required.

Pack the unfilled Pavlova in a protective box to freeze.

SPEEDY BAKED ALASKA

S E R V E S

—— 6–8 ——

600-ml (1-pint) tub vanilla
    ice-cream
18-cm (7-inch) sponge flan
    case
215-g (7 ½-oz) can apricot
    halves in natural juice or
    other canned fruit
1 tablespoon brandy
Icing sugar for dusting

FOR THE MERINGUE TOPPING
2 egg whites
100 g (4 oz) caster sugar
A few flaked almonds

Try to buy good quality ice-cream in a round tub – but not soft scoop – as opposed to a block for this recipe. That way no shaping of the ice-cream is necessary, simply invert it onto the flan case.

Pre-heat the oven to gas mark 8, 450°F (230°C). Allow the ice-cream to soften slightly in the refrigerator. Place the sponge flan case in a shallow freezer- and oven-proof dish. Drain the apricots, reserving the juice, and arrange over the flan case. Mix 1 tablespoon of the reserved juice with the brandy and sprinkle over the fruit.

Run a knife in-between the ice-cream and the container and invert onto the apricots in the flan case. Place in the freezer whilst the meringue is being made.

To make the meringue: whisk the egg whites until they stand in soft peaks. Gradually whisk in the sugar, a teaspoon at a time keeping the mixture stiff. Once all the sugar has been added it should be stiff, smooth and shiny.

Spoon the meringue all over the sponge flan and the ice-cream to enclose both completely. Swirl the meringue with the back of a spoon to form peaks and sprinkle with a few flaked almonds.

Bake immediately for 3–4 minutes or until well browned. Dust with icing sugar and cut into wedges to serve.

TIRAMISU

SERVES

—— 8 ——

L ook out for the soft Italian sponge fingers or *savoiardi* which are available from good delicatessens to replace the trifle sponges. This dessert freezes well.

▬▬▬▬▬▬

Line a 20–23-cm (8–9-inch) loose-bottomed round cake tin, or spring release tin, with non-stick baking parchment. Dissolve the coffee in the boiling water and mix with the brandy.

Break the eggs into a bowl, add the sugar and whisk together at high speed until thick and frothy – the mixture should leave its own trail when trickled from a height. Mix a little of this mixture with the cheese in another bowl, then stir in the remaining egg and sugar mixture.

Whisk the cream until thick and fold into the egg and Mascarpone mixture. Coarsely chop the chocolate chips in a food processor to give chocolate bits and powder.

Split the sponge fingers and line the prepared tin with half of them. Sprinkle over half the coffee mixture and scatter over one third of the chocolate then add half of the Mascarpone mixture. Add the second layer of sponge, then the remaining coffee mixture and another third of the chocolate. Cover with the rest of the Mascarpone mixture and sprinkle with the remaining chocolate.

Chill for 4 hours then turn out of the tin, remove the paper and serve very cold.

INGREDIENTS

1 generous teaspoon instant coffee
120 ml (4 fl oz) boiling water
85 ml (3 fl oz) brandy
2 eggs
65 g (2 ½ oz) caster sugar
250 g (9 oz) Mascarpone soft Italian cheese
300 ml (10 fl oz) double cream
75 g (3 oz) chocolate chips
1 packet trifle sponges

GUERNSEY APPLE CAKE

———— • ————

225 g (8 oz) self-raising brown flour
Grated rind of 1 lemon
1 teaspoon baking powder
100 g (4 oz) margarine
225 g (8 oz) light muscovado sugar
2 eggs
175 g (6 oz) (prepared) peeled, cored and chopped cooking apples
Icing sugar for dusting

A wonderful way to use up a glut of apples, this cake is best served warm with whipped cream. Expect it to dip in the middle a little.

Pre-heat the oven to gas mark 3, 325°F (160°C). Grease and base line a deep 18-cm (7-inch) round cake tin with greased greaseproof paper.

Measure the flour, lemon rind, baking powder, margarine, sugar and eggs into a bowl and mix together until evenly blended and smooth. Fold in the prepared apples.

Spoon the mixture into the prepared tin and bake for about 1–1¼ hours or until well risen and the surface springs back when lightly pressed with a finger.

Allow to cool in the tin for about 10 minutes before turning out to cool completely on a wire rack. Dust with icing sugar and eat within 1–2 days.

Raspberry meringue roulade

SERVES
—— 8 ——

This meringue freezes well, so you can make it in advance if necessary. Simply wrap in foil to freeze, then allow 6 hours to thaw before serving.

———

Pre-heat the oven to gas mark 7, 425°F (220°C). Line a 33 × 23 cm (13 × 9 inch) Swiss roll tin with greased non-stick baking parchment.

Whisk the egg whites until very stiff. Gradually add the sugar a teaspoon at a time, whisking well between each addition. Whisk until very, very stiff and all the sugar has been included. (This will take about 10 minutes with an electric mixer.) Spread the meringue mixture into the lined tin and sprinkle with the almonds.

Place the tin fairly near the top of the oven and bake for about 8 minutes until very golden and firm to the touch.

Whisk the cream until it stands in stiff peaks and mix in the raspberries. Remove the meringue from the oven and turn almond side-down onto a sheet of non-stick baking parchment. Remove the paper from the base of the cooked meringue and allow to cool for about 8 minutes.

Spread the cream and raspberries evenly over the meringue. Start to roll from the long end fairly tightly until rolled up like a roulade. Wrap in non-stick baking parchment and chill before serving.

INGREDIENTS

4 egg whites
225 g (8 oz) caster sugar
40 g (1 ½ oz) flaked almonds
300 ml (10 fl oz) double cream
225 g (8 oz) raspberries

STRAWBERRY PAVLOVA

SERVES

—— 6–8 ——

A great luxury and a top favourite with all ages. Traditionally the inside of the meringue is soft and marshmallow-like and the outside is crisp.

INGREDIENTS

3 egg whites
175 g (6 oz) caster sugar
1 teaspoon cornflour
1 teaspoon white wine
    vinegar
FOR THE FILLING
300 ml (10 fl oz) whipping
    cream, whipped
225 g (8 oz) strawberries

Pre-heat the oven to gas mark 3, 325°F (160°C). Lay a sheet of non-stick baking parchment on a baking tray and mark a 20-cm (8-inch) circle on it.

Whisk the egg whites until stiff, then add the sugar a teaspoonful at a time, whilst still whisking at full speed. Blend the cornflour and vinegar together and whisk into the meringue mixture. Spread the meringue out to cover the circle on the baking tray, building up the sides so they are higher than the middle.

Place in the oven but immediately reduce the temperature to gas mark 2, 300°F (150°C). Bake the pavlova for about 1 hour until firm to the touch and a pale beige colour. Turn the oven off and allow the pavlova to become quite cold while still in the oven.

Remove the pavlova from the baking tray and paper and slide onto a serving plate. Fill with the whipped cream and strawberries. Leave the pavlova in the refrigerator for 1 hour before serving.

GINGER CREAM ROLL

S E R V E S

—— 4–6 ——

C ouldn't be simpler ... a real cheat! However, it does need to be made the day before serving.

Put half the whipping cream in a bowl and whisk until it forms fairly stiff peaks.

Quickly dip each biscuit in a little brandy and then sandwich together with cream shaping into a long roll. Place on a serving dish and leave in the refrigerator overnight.

The next day, whip the remaining cream and use it to cover the roll completely and to pipe rosettes down the length of the roll. Decorate with slices of stem ginger.

To serve, cut the roll in diagonal slices.

INGREDIENTS

450 ml (15 fl oz) whipping cream
225 g (8 oz) ginger biscuits
4 tablespoons brandy
Slices of stem ginger to decorate

BRANDY CHOCOLATE CHARLOTTE

SERVES

—— 8 ——

*About 20 sponge fingers
(Boudoir biscuits)*
3 tablespoons brandy

FOR THE MOUSSE
100 g (4 oz) plain chocolate
2 eggs
*175 g (6 oz) soft unsalted
butter*
150 g (5 oz) caster sugar

TO DECORATE
*150 ml (5 fl oz) whipping
cream*
Grated chocolate

This is very rich so the slices are quite small. The loaf shape is easy to serve. You'll need to prepare this a day in advance.

First line a 900-g (2-lb) loaf tin with greaseproof paper: dip each Boudoir biscuit, sugar side down, in the brandy and arrange about 8–9 sugar side down on the base of the loaf tin. Cut the remaining Boudoir biscuits in half and dip, sugar side-down, in the brandy and stand them, sugar side out, around the edge of the tin.

Then make the mousse: break the chocolate into pieces and place in a small bowl over a pan of simmering water and allow to melt slowly. Put the melted chocolate, eggs, butter and sugar in a food processor and blend until smooth. Alternatively, beat well with a whisk. Turn into the loaf tin and smooth the top. Chill overnight.

The next day turn out onto a serving dish. Whisk the cream until thick, then pipe rosettes on the Charlotte. Decorate with grated chocolate.

FAST CHEESECAKES

The cheesecake originated in Russia and Eastern Europe well over a century ago and used local soft cheese, sugar and eggs baked in a pastry case.

Today, cooked and uncooked cheesecakes are popular, the chilled cheesecakes (originally from America) are usually set with gelatine and lighter in texture than the European baked varieties.

These cheesecakes are very simple to make but some will need to be made the day before serving. Don't be put off by the use of gelatine in a recipe, by following a few basic guidelines it is bound to work.

● Buy powdered gelatine which is ready weighed in packets to prevent problems with weighing small amounts accurately.

● To 'sponge' gelatine, always sprinkle the gelatine over the water in a small bowl or cup, and not the other way round or you will get lumpy gelatine.

● Allowing the gelatine to 'sponge' before melting helps it to dissolve more evenly.

● Gelatine must be dissolved carefully. Heat gently by standing the bowl of 'sponged' gelatine over a pan of gently simmering water and do not allow to boil.

● The gelatine is ready to use when it is absolutely clear.

Cheesecakes are best made in a spring release tin to make turning out easy, but if you do not own one a cake tin with a loose base works almost as well.

It is very easy to vary the flavours of cheesecakes. Use ½ pint of sweetened fruit puree such as raspberry, strawberry, blackcurrant or gooseberry to replace the apricot and orange in the *Apricot and Orange Hob-Nob Cheesecake* for instance.

LAURA'S AMERICAN CHEESECAKE

SERVES
— 8 —

450 g (1 lb) low-fat soft cheese
150 g (5 oz) caster sugar
50 g (2 oz) unsalted butter, at room temperature
25 g (1 oz) cornflour
Juice and rind of 2 lemons
3 eggs
300 ml (10 fl oz) double cream
Soft fruits to decorate (optional)

There is no need to use a full-fat cheese for this recipe as the butter and the double cream add sufficient richness. Our American neighbour Laura won second prize in our local village show with this recipe. Don't be surprised that this cheesecake doesn't have a base – it makes it much lighter.

Pre-heat the oven to gas mark 4, 350°F (180°C). Lightly grease and base line a 20-cm (8-inch) round loose-bottomed cake tin with greased greaseproof paper.

Place the cheese, sugar, butter, cornflour, lemon rind and juice and eggs into a large bowl. Beat thoroughly to mix until smooth. Lightly whip the double cream and fold into the cheese mixture.

Pour into the prepared tin and bake in a bain-marie (a roasting tin half-filled with hot water) for about 1 hour or until set and golden. Turn off the oven and allow the cheesecake to cool before removing.

Remove from the oven, cool completely, then refrigerate to set. Decorate with soft fruits if desired. Cut and serve in wedges.

*E*ASY
LEMON CHEESECAKE

S E R V E S
—— 6 ——

A real cheat but so delicious!

Mix together the crushed biscuits, butter and demerara sugar to make the biscuit base. Turn into a 20-cm (8-inch) flan dish and press evenly over the base and sides. Leave to set.

For the cheesecake filling: mix together the cream, con-densed milk, soft cheese and lemon rind, then add the lemon juice a little at a time, whisking until the mixture thickens. Pour the mixture into the flan case and leave to chill in the refrigerator for 3–4 hours, or overnight.

Decorate with swirls of whipped cream and a few fresh strawberries or grapes as desired.

INGREDIENTS

FOR THE BASE
10 digestive biscuits, crushed
50 g (2 oz) butter, melted
25 g (1 oz) demerara sugar

FOR THE CHEESECAKE
150 ml (5 fl oz) single cream
1 × 400 g (14 oz) can condensed milk
100 g (4 oz) low-fat soft cheese, softened
Grated rind and juice of 2 large lemons

FOR THE TOPPING
150 ml (5 fl oz) whipping cream, whipped
A few fresh strawberries or grapes to decorate

GERMAN CHEESECAKE

S E R V E S
— 6 —

A rich, moist cheesecake. Don't worry if the sultanas sink whilst the cheesecake is baking.

FOR THE BASE

4 digestive biscuits, crushed
15 g (½ oz) demerara sugar
25 g (1 oz) butter, melted

FOR THE CHEESECAKE

3 eggs
100 g (4 oz) caster sugar
450 g (1 lb) full-fat cream
cheese, at room
temperature
Finely grated rind of 1 large
lemon
175 g (6 oz) sultanas

TO FINISH

Icing sugar for dusting

Pre-heat the oven to gas mark 4, 350°F (180°C). Lightly butter and flour an 18-cm (7-inch) round loose-bottomed cake tin, or spring release tin.

Mix together the ingredients for the biscuit base, spread over the base of the tin and press down firmly with the back of a metal spoon.

Put the ingredients for the cheesecake into a bowl and mix until well blended and smooth. Pour on top of the crumb base and then bake for about 1½ hours, or until well risen, pale golden brown and shrinking slightly away from the sides of the tin.

Turn off the heat and leave the cheesecake in the oven for a further 15 minutes. Then remove the cheesecake from the oven and leave to cool in the tin. When cold, remove from the tin and chill in the refrigerator until required.

Dust with sieved icing sugar before serving.

CONTINENTAL CHEESECAKE

SERVES

—— 10 ——

A traditional cooked cheesecake. Expect the sides of the cake to be a little higher than the centre after baking – it gives a nice dip to take the blackcurrant or cherry topping.

Pre-heat the oven to gas mark 3, 325°F (160°C). Lightly oil a 23-cm (9-inch) loose-bottomed round cake tin, and line base and sides with greased greaseproof paper.

Mix together the ingredients for the base, spread over the base of the tin and press down firmly with the back of a metal spoon. Leave to set.

Measure the margarine, sugar, curd cheese, flour, rind and juice of the lemon, and the egg yolks into a large bowl. Beat until smooth. Fold in the cream. Whisk the egg whites until stiff then fold into the mixture. Pour onto the biscuit crust.

Bake for about 1 hour or until set. Turn off the oven and leave the cheesecake in the oven for a further hour to cool. Run a knife around the edge of the tin to loosen the cheesecake and push the base up through the cake tin. Remove the side paper.

For the topping: place the fruit with its juice in a small saucepan. Dissolve the arrowroot in a little cold water and mix into the fruit. Bring up to the boil to thicken the juice, adding a dash of kirsch for flavour, if desired. Allow to cool completely, then pile on top of the cheesecake.

Decorate the edge of the cheesecake with piped or spooned whipped double cream.

INGREDIENTS

FOR THE BASE
75 g (3 oz) digestive
  biscuits, crushed
40 g (1 ½ oz) butter, melted
25 g (1 oz) demerara sugar

FOR THE CHEESECAKE
50 g (2 oz) soft margarine
175 g (6 oz) caster sugar
450 g (1 lb) curd cheese
25 g (1 oz) plain flour
Finely grated rind and juice
  of 1 lemon
3 eggs, separated
150 ml (5 fl oz) double
  cream, lightly whipped

FOR THE TOPPING
1 × 425-g (15-oz) can
  blackcurrants or stoned
  black cherries
1 heaped teaspoon arrowroot
A little kirsch (optional)
150 ml (5 fl oz) double
  cream, whipped, to
  decorate

APRICOT AND ORANGE HOB-NOB CHEESECAKE

SERVES

—— 10 ——

P owdered gelatine is easy to use providing you soak it in cold water to form a sponge first.

FOR THE BASE
50 g (2 oz) butter
25 g (1 oz) demerara sugar
100 g (4 oz) Hob-Nobs,
  coarsely crushed

FOR THE CHEESECAKE
15-g (½-oz) packet powdered
  gelatine
4 tablespoons water
175 g (6 oz) ready-soaked
  dried apricots
200 ml (7 fl oz) fresh orange
  juice
3 tablespoons clear honey
225 g (8 oz) full-fat cream
  cheese
150 ml (5 fl oz) soured
  cream
2 eggs, separated
100 g (4 oz) caster sugar

FOR THE TOPPING
1 tablespoon apricot jam,
  heated and sieved
150 ml (5 fl oz) whipping
  cream, whipped
10 small ratafia biscuits

Melt the butter for the base, add the demerara sugar and the coarsely crushed biscuits. Mix together and use to line a loose-bottomed 23-cm (9-inch) round cake tin.

In a small bowl, sprinkle the gelatine over the water and leave to 'sponge'. Place the apricots in a pan with the orange juice, bring to the boil then simmer gently for about 5 minutes or until the apricots are tender. Turn into a food processor and add the honey, cream cheese, soured cream and egg yolks. Process together until well mixed and smooth. Or, push the apricots through a nylon sieve, then mix with the honey, cream cheese, soured cream and egg yolks.

Stand the bowl of gelatine in a pan of gently simmering water and allow to dissolve. Mix into the apricot mixture in the processor or by hand.

Whisk the egg whites until frothy, add the caster sugar a little at a time until all is incorporated and the mixture is very stiff. Turn the apricot mixture into the meringue mixture and fold well together. Pour onto the biscuit crust and chill in the fridge to set.

Loosen the side edges of the tin using a small palette knife if necessary. Push up the base of the tin and slip the cheesecake onto a serving plate. Spread over the warmed apricot jam, mark into 10 wedges. Spoon a blob of cream onto each wedge, and place a ratafia biscuit on each section of cheesecake. Serve chilled.

CHOCOLATE, RUM AND RAISIN CHEESECAKE

S E R V E S
—— 8 ——

The raisins do need to be soaked overnight in the rum, but once that is done this cheesecake takes no time at all to prepare.

———

Soak the raisins for the cheesecake in the rum overnight.

Slip the sponge flan case into a greased loose-bottomed 20-cm (8-inch) round cake tin, or spring release tin, trimming the cake if necessary to fit.

Break the chocolate into small pieces and place in a bowl. Gently melt the chocolate by placing the bowl over a pan of simmering water. Allow to cool slightly.

In a small bowl, sprinkle the gelatine over the water. Leave to 'sponge', then stand the bowl over a pan of gently simmering water until the gelatine has completely dissolved.

Beat together the egg yolks, sugar and cheese in a large bowl. Add the soured cream and cooled chocolate. Stir in the dissolved gelatine. Whisk the egg whites until frothy and fold into the cheese mixture with the soaked raisins. Pour onto the sponge base and refrigerate to set.

Carefully remove the cheesecake from the tin before decorating with whipped cream, chocolate curls and raisins.

INGREDIENTS

FOR THE BASE
1 sponge flan case, about 20 cm (8 inches) in diameter

FOR THE CHEESECAKE
50 g (2 oz) seedless raisins
4 tablespoons rum
100 g (4 oz) plain chocolate
15 g (½ oz) packet powdered gelatine
3 tablespoons cold water
2 eggs, separated
50 g (2 oz) caster sugar
225 g (8 oz) full-fat soft cheese
150 ml (5 fl oz) soured cream

FOR THE TOPPING
150 ml (5 fl oz) whipping cream, whipped
Chocolate curls to decorate
Raisins to decorate

ORANGE JAFFA CHEESECAKE

S E R V E S
—— 8 ——

A very smooth, fresh cheesecake – the ginger biscuits go really well with the orange. The easiest cheesecake to make but you'll need to leave about 30 minutes for the jelly to almost set.

FOR THE BASE

100 g (4 oz) ginger biscuits, crushed
50 g (2 oz) butter, melted
25 g (1 oz) demerara sugar

FOR THE CHEESECAKE

600-ml (1-pint) packet orange jelly
150 ml (5 fl oz) Jaffa breakfast orange juice
350 g (12 oz) full-fat cream cheese
100 g (4 oz) caster sugar
150 ml (5 fl oz) whipping cream, whipped

FOR THE TOPPING

Small can mandarin oranges in natural juice
Sprigs of fresh mint (optional)

Lightly grease a 20-cm (8-inch) round loose-bottomed cake tin or spring release tin.

Dissolve the jelly in 150 ml (5 fl oz) boiling water then add the orange juice to make it up to 300 ml (10 fl oz). Put in a cold place until the jelly is thick and nearly set.

Meanwhile, mix together the ingredients for the base and spread over the base of the prepared tin, pressing down firmly.

Mix the cream cheese with the sugar and the almost set jelly and then fold in the whipped cream. Turn into the tin on top of the biscuit crumbs and put in a cool place to set.

To serve, loosen the sides of the cheesecake from the tin and push up the base, or remove the sides of the spring release tin and slide the cheesecake onto a plate. Drain the mandarin oranges and place around the edge of the cheesecake to decorate. Add sprigs of fresh mint if desired.

ALMOND CHEESECAKE TARTLETS

MAKES

—— about 18 ——

A few sultanas can be added to the cheese filling as a variation for this recipe.

————

Pre-heat the oven to gas mark 5, 375°F (190°C).

First make the pastry. Place the flour into a bowl and rub in the margarine until the mixture resembles fine breadcrumbs. Bind to a dough with the water. Roll out the pastry thinly on a lightly floured surface and, using a 7.5-cm (3-inch) fluted cutter, stamp out about 18 rounds. Place in bun tins and chill.

Whisk together the cheese, margarine, eggs, lemon juice and grated rind, sugar, ground almonds and almond essence.

Divide the cheese mixture between the tartlets, filling them almost to the brim. Bake for about 25–30 minutes, or until just set and golden. Cool in the tins for about 5 minutes before easing out to cool on a wire rack. Eat really fresh.

INGREDIENTS

FOR THE SHORTCRUST
  PASTRY
175 g (6 oz) plain flour
75 g (3 oz) margarine
2–3 tablespoons cold water

FOR THE FILLING
100 g (4 oz) curd cheese
50 g (2 oz) soft margarine
2 eggs
*Juice and grated rind of 1
  lemon*
50 g (2 oz) caster sugar
25 g (1 oz) ground almonds
Few drops almond essence

LIME CHEESECAKE

S E R V E S

—— about 20 ——

This is a really good party cheesecake.

FOR THE BASE
100 g (4 oz) butter
50 g (2 oz) demerara sugar
*225 g (8 oz) digestive
   biscuits, crushed*

FOR THE CHEESECAKE
4 limes
*25 g (1 oz) powdered
   gelatine*
4 tablespoons water
*450 g (1 lb) full fat cream
   cheese*
*300 ml (10 fl oz) Greek
   yogurt*
4 eggs, separated
225 g (8 oz) caster sugar

TO DECORATE
*150 ml (5 fl oz) whipping
   cream, whipped*
Strawberries and limes

Lightly grease a 28 cm (11 inch) spring release tin or round loose bottomed cake tin with oil.

Measure the butter for the base into a pan and heat until melted. Add the demerara sugar and the crushed digestive biscuits and mix together. Spoon into the base of the prepared tin and flatten with a metal spoon. Chill whilst making the filling.

Finely grate the limes, then squeeze the juice into a small bowl (there should be about 4 tablespoons juice out of 4 limes). Add 4 tablespoons of water to the bowl then sprinkle over the gelatine. Leave to sponge for about 10 minutes, then stand the bowl in a pan of simmering water and heat gently until the gelatine has dissolved.

Measure the cheese, Greek yogurt, egg yolks and the grated rind of the limes into a bowl or food processor and mix until smooth. Gradually pour in the dissolved gelatine and mix well.

Whisk the egg whites in a separate bowl until frothy, then add the caster sugar a little at a time, whisking continuously until the mixture is very stiff. Turn the lime and cheese mixture into the meringue mixture and blend well together. Pour onto the biscuit crust, cover and chill until set.

Loosen the set cheesecake from the sides of the tin and push up or remove the base. Slide onto a serving plate and decorate with rosettes of whipped cream, strawberries and fine slices of lime.

Serve chilled.

TRAYBAKES

These are the fastest and easiest cakes of all to make. No special tins are needed: the cake is cooked, cooled and iced in an oblong roasting tin. There is no need to turn the cake out onto a cooling rack (less washing up!) and no icing is wasted dribbling down the sides of the cake onto the work surface, only to need mopping up. Simply cut the cake into squares, triangles or fingers for children's parties, large family gatherings or fund-raising events.

All of the recipes which follow use the one basic traybake sponge with slight variations to give different flavours. Experiment yourself using the same formula to create your family's favourites.

BASIC ALL-IN-ONE SPONGE TRAYBAKE

— • —

175 g (6 oz) soft margarine
175 g (6 oz) caster sugar
225 g (8 oz) self-raising
  flour
1 ½ teaspoons baking powder
3 eggs
3 tablespoons milk

This recipe, with all its variations, must be one of the most useful. It's ideal for large families or children's parties because it's so quick and easy to prepare and so versatile.

Pre-heat the oven to gas mark 4, 350°F (180°C). Grease and base line a roasting tin about 30 × 23 cm (12 × 9 inches) with greased greaseproof paper.

Measure the margarine, sugar, flour, baking powder, eggs and milk together in a large bowl and beat well for about 2 minutes until well blended. Turn the mixture into the pre-pared tin and level the top. Bake for about 30–35 minutes, or until the cake has shrunk from the sides of the tin and springs back when pressed in the centre with your fingertips. Leave to cool in the tin and cut into 21 pieces.

*I*CED
LEMON TRAYBAKE

—— • ——

P re-heat the oven, prepare the roasting tin and make the sponge mixture as on page 94, adding the lemon rind to the cake ingredients. Bake for 30–35 minutes.

   Allow the baked cake to cool. Then, mix together the lemon juice and sieved icing sugar until smooth, adding a little more lemon juice if necessary to give a runny consistency. Spread out evenly over the cake and leave to set, before cutting into squares or triangles.

INGREDIENTS

175 g (6 oz) soft margarine
175 g (6 oz) caster sugar
225 g (8 oz) self-raising
   flour
1 ½ teaspoons baking powder
3 eggs
3 tablespoons milk
Grated rind of 1 ½ lemons

FOR THE ICING

About 3 tablespoons lemon
   juice
225 g (8 oz) icing sugar

CHOCOLATE MARBLE TRAYBAKE

INGREDIENTS

175 g (6 oz) soft margarine
175 g (6 oz) caster sugar
225 g (8 oz) self-raising
  flour
1 ½ teaspoons baking powder
3 eggs
3 tablespoons milk
1 tablespoons cocoa
1 tablespoon hot water
Sieved icing sugar for dusting

P re-heat the oven, prepare the roasting tin and make up the basic traybake sponge mixture as on page 94. Place half of the mixture in teaspoonfuls over the base of the prepared tin. Mix together the cocoa and hot water and beat into the remaining cake mixture. Spoon this mixture into the tin between the spoonfuls of plain mixture and swirl a little with a knife to level the surface.

Bake for 30–35 minutes. Sprinkle the cooked, cooled cake with sieved icing sugar.

ICED
CHOCOLATE TRAYBAKE

— • —

Pre-heat the oven and prepare the roasting tin and basic sponge recipe as on page 94. Blend the 3 tablespoons cocoa with the hot water and allow to cool slightly. Add to the basic all-in-one sponge mixture but omit completely or only use 1 tablespoon of the milk in the recipe if necessary.

Bake for 30–35 minutes. Leave the cake to cool in the tin.

For the icing: melt the margarine in a small saucepan and then stir in the sieved cocoa and cook over a gentle heat for 1 minute. Remove from the heat and then stir in the sieved icing sugar and milk. Beat well until the icing has thickened and then spread over the cooled cake. Leave to set before cutting into squares or triangles.

INGREDIENTS

3 tablespoons cocoa
3 tablespoons hot water
175 g (6 oz) soft margarine
175 g (6 oz) caster sugar
225 g (8 oz) self-raising
   flour
1 ½ teaspoons baking powder
3 eggs
1 tablespoon milk (optional)

FOR THE ICING
75 g (3 oz) margarine
50 g (2 oz) cocoa, sieved
225 g (8 oz) icing sugar,
   sieved
2 tablespoons milk

BAKEWELL TART TRAYBAKE

•

FOR THE SHORTCRUST
    PASTRY
175 g (6 oz) plain flour
75 g (3 oz) margarine
2–3 tablespoons cold water

FOR THE SPONGE MIXTURE
100 g (4 oz) soft margarine
100 g (4 oz) caster sugar
175 g (6 oz) self-raising
    flour
1 teaspoon baking powder
2 eggs
2 tablespoons milk
½ teaspoon almond essence

About 4 tablespoons
    raspberry jam
Flaked almonds for
    sprinkling

Be generous with the raspberry jam, it makes all the difference. There's no need to line the tin with greaseproof paper for this pastry traybake, because the pastry already contains a lot of fat and no sugar to make it stick.

First make the pastry. Place the flour in a bowl and rub in the margarine until the mixture resembles fine breadcrumbs. Bind to a dough with the water. Roll out the pastry on a lightly floured surface and line a roasting tin 30 × 23 cm (12 × 9 inches) with it.

Then pre-heat the oven, and make up the basic sponge mixture as on page 94, adding the almond essence.

Spread the pastry with plenty of raspberry jam and then top with the sponge mixture. Sprinkle with the flaked almonds and bake for about 25 minutes.

CHERRY AND APRICOT TRAYBAKE

———— • ————

B utter is used in place of the margarine in this traybake to give it a really special flavour. Make sure the butter is at room temperature before you start mixing. Nibbed sugar is what bakers use on top of Bath buns.

━━━

Pre-heat the oven, prepare the roasting tin and make the basic sponge mixture as on page 94, adding the prepared glacé cherries and apricots.

Bake for 30–35 minutes, sprinkling the nibbed sugar or crushed sugar cubes over the cake three-quarters of the way through the cooking time.

175 g (6 oz) butter
175 g (6 oz) caster sugar
225 g (8 oz) self-raising flour
1 ½ teaspoons baking powder
3 eggs
3 tablespoons milk
75 g (3 oz) glacé cherries, quartered, washed and dried
75 g (3 oz) no-soak dried apricots, cut into small pieces
2 tablespoons nibbed sugar or crushed sugar cubes

FRUIT TRAYBAKE

———— • ————

INGREDIENTS

175 g (6 oz) soft margarine
175 g (6 oz) caster sugar
225 g (8 oz) self-raising
  flour
1 ½ teaspoons baking powder
3 eggs
3 tablespoons milk
225 g (8 oz) currants
2 tablespoons demerara sugar

P re-heat the oven, prepare the roasting tin and make the basic sponge mixture as on page 94, adding the currants to the other ingredients in the bowl.

Bake for 30–35 minutes, sprinkling the demerara sugar over the cake three-quarters of the way through the cooking time to give a crunchy topping.

COFFEE FUDGE SQUARES

———— • ————

While it is best to use coffee essence in terms of flavour and colour, you can use a mixture of 2 teaspoons of instant coffee and 1 tablespoon of hot water for each table-spoon of coffee essence.

Pre-heat the oven, prepare the roasting tin and make the basic sponge mixture as on page 94 adding the coffee essence. Bake for 30–35 minutes.

For the fudge topping: put the butter, muscovado sugar and milk into a small pan and heat gently until the sugar dissolves. Then boil briskly for 3 minutes. Remove from the heat and gradually stir in the sieved icing sugar. Beat thoroughly until smooth. Spread quickly over the top of the baked cake and sprinkle over the chopped walnuts.

INGREDIENTS

175 g (6 oz) soft margarine
175 g (6 oz) caster sugar
225 g (8 oz) self-raising
  flour
1 ½ teaspoons baking powder
3 eggs
2 tablespoons milk
1 tablespoon coffee essence
FOR THE TOPPING
50 g (2 oz) butter
100 g (4 oz) light brown
  muscovado sugar
2 tablespoons milk
275 g (10 oz) icing sugar,
  sieved
25 g (1 oz) chopped walnuts

MINCEMEAT AND ALMOND BAKE

———— • ————

INGREDIENTS

FOR THE SHORTCRUST PASTRY

175 g (6 oz) plain flour
75 g (3 oz) margarine
2–3 tablespoons cold water

3 generous tablespoons mincemeat
2 egg whites
6 tablespoons ground almonds
100 g (4 oz) caster sugar
Few drops almond essence
50 g (2 oz) slivered or chopped almonds

Pre-heat the oven to gas mark 4, 350°F (180°C).
Place the flour in a bowl and rub in the margarine until the mixture resembles fine breadcrumbs. Bind to a dough with the water. Roll out on a lightly floured surface and line a 30 × 25 cm (12 × 9-inch) roasting tin with it. Spread with the mincemeat.

Whisk the egg whites until stiff but not dry, fold in the ground almonds, caster sugar and a few drops of almond essence. Spread this mixture over the mincemeat. Sprinkle with the slivered or chopped almonds and bake for about 25 minutes until crisp and golden. Cool in the tin.

Opposite: ORANGE JAFFA CHEESECAKE (*Page 90*)

Overleaf: FARMHOUSE ORANGE VICTORIA SANDWICH (*Page 126*)

N O - B A K E   C A K E S

A delicious cake made without even turning the oven on has got to be a bonus. They're ideal for children to make themselves because these cakes simply involve melting ingredients together and setting them in the fridge for an hour or so, if the sticky fingers can wait that long!

It is best to eat no-bake cakes when they're as fresh as possible, they really won't keep for very long. So make sure everyone's hungry before you decide to try any of these recipes.

ICE-CREAM CAKE

S E R V E S

—— 8 ——

INGREDIENTS

1-litre (1 ¾-pint) carton vanilla ice-cream (not soft scoop)
400-g (14-oz) can any fruit in natural juice
About 24 sponge fingers (Boudoir biscuits)
Chocolate flake to decorate
Candles and ribbon to finish

This can be an instant birthday cake as it is so quick to prepare and children always love ice-cream. Make on the day, or prepare it a week ahead and keep in the freezer.

Line the base of a 20-cm (8-inch) round shallow loose-bottomed cake tin or spring release tin with greaseproof paper.

Leave the ice-cream at room-temperature for about 15 minutes to soften. Drain the canned fruit, reserving the juice. Dip the sponge fingers into the juice, then arrange the fingers over the base and sides of the tin, halving the biscuits to go around the side.

Arrange the drained fruit over the biscuits on the base of the tin in a single layer. Scoop out the softened ice-cream and fill the cake tin. Smooth over the surface and freeze until firm.

Turn the cake out onto a serving plate and decorate the top edge with broken chocolate flake. Tie a ribbon around the side of the cake and place candles in the top.

Chocolate terrine

S E R V E S
—— 8–10 ——

M ake this the day before you need it as it does need to be chilled overnight in the refrigerator. Serve very cold, even half frozen, and in very thin slices.

———

Line a 900-g (2-lb) loaf tin with foil.

Break the chocolate into small pieces and place in a pan with the margarine. Heat gently until melted. Beat the eggs and sugar together until blended, then gradually add the chocolate mixture a little at a time.

Break the biscuits into 1-cm (½-inch) pieces and stir into the chocolate mixture. Pack into the tin and smooth the top. Leave to set in the refrigerator overnight.

Turn out onto a serving dish and peel off the foil. Decorate with the whipped cream and chocolate buttons or Maltesers.

INGREDIENTS

225 g (8 oz) milk chocolate
225 g (8 oz) margarine
2 eggs
25 g (1 oz) caster sugar
225 g (8 oz) Nice biscuits
*150 ml (5 fl oz) double
  cream, whipped*
*Chocolate buttons or
  Maltesers to decorate*

TOFFEE AND MARSHMALLOW SQUARES

M A K E S

—— about 20 ——

100g (4oz) hard margarine
100g (4oz) marshmallows
100g (4oz) dairy toffees
200g (7oz) rice krispies

This is very popular with all children – something that can be made by very young children with supervision. My daughter Annabel still makes them and she is well past being a teenager!

Measure the margarine, marshmallows and toffees into a thick-based saucepan and heat gently until the mixture is melted and smooth. This will take about 5 minutes.

Place the rice krispies in a bowl. Pour over the toffee mixture and stir well to mix.

Spoon into an oblong tin, about 30 × 23 cm (12 × 9 inches) and press flat. Leave in a cool place until set and quite firm and then cut into squares.

NUT AND SULTANA TIFFIN

M A K E S

—— 12 bars ——

I deal to pack for a picnic or lunchbox.

Lightly grease a shallow 18-cm (7-inch) square tin.

Melt the syrup, butter and chocolate in a heatproof bowl over a pan of hot water.

Add the crushed biscuits, walnuts and sultanas and mix well. Spoon into the prepared tin and level the surface. Chill until set, then cut into 12 bars.

INGREDIENTS

2 tablespoons golden syrup

75 g (3 oz) butter

50 g (2 oz) plain chocolate

100 g (4 oz) digestive biscuits, crushed

50 g (2 oz) rich tea biscuits, crushed

50 g (2 oz) walnuts, chopped

75 g (3 oz) sultanas

HONEY FUDGE WEDGES

MAKES

—— about 16 ——

175g (6 oz) hard margarine
6 tablespoons clear honey
225g (8 oz) currants
50g (2 oz) glacé cherries,
    quartered
50g (2 oz) raisins
350g (12 oz) digestive,
    Nice or rich tea biscuits,
    crushed

Use up any broken biscuits at the bottom of the tin for this recipe.

Lightly grease a 20-cm (8-inch) round loose-bottomed, or spring release cake tin.

Heat the margarine and honey in a pan over a low heat until the margarine has melted. Increase the heat and boil rapidly for about 2 minutes, whisking all the time. Remove from the heat and allow to cool.

Place all the remaining ingredients into a large bowl, add the melted mixture and stir thoroughly to mix. Press into the prepared tin and level out evenly.

Chill thoroughly before serving in thin wedges.

PASSION SPONGE

S E R V E S
—— 4–6 ——

A variation of my ever-popular passion pudding. It takes all of 5 minutes to make!

———

Place the sponge flan case on a serving plate. Drain the raspberries, saving the juice, and spoon them evenly over the flan case. Spoon over a little of the reserved juice with a splash of the liqueur if desired.

Whisk the double cream until stiff then fold in the Greek yoghurt. Pile on top of the raspberries. Sprinkle over the sugar and chill until the sugar has melted into the topping.

INGREDIENTS

18–20-cm (7–8-inch) sponge flan case

400-g (14-oz) can raspberries in natural juice

A little framboise or cassis liqueur (optional)

150 ml (5 fl oz) double cream

225 g (8 oz) Greek yoghurt

1–2 tablespoons light soft brown sugar

ICED KRISPIE BARS

MAKES
—— about 28 ——

225 g (8 oz) milk chocolate
100 g (4 oz) margarine
25 g (1 oz) desiccated
   coconut
75 g (3 oz) rice krispies

FOR THE ICING

225 g (8 oz) icing sugar,
   sieved
About 4 tablespoons lemon
   juice
Chocolate buttons to decorate

B est eaten and made on the same day.

Lightly grease a Swiss roll tin, 33 × 23 cm (13 × 9 inches).
   Break the chocolate into pieces into a roomy bowl and add the margarine. Place the bowl over a pan of simmering water and gently melt the chocolate and margarine together. Off the heat stir in the coconut and rice krispies. Mix thoroughly then spread the mixture into the prepared tin and leave to set.
   For the icing: add enough lemon juice to the icing sugar to make a coating consistency. Spread the icing over the set krispie mixture and decorate with the chocolate buttons. Leave to set before cutting into bars.

CAKES THAT CHILDREN
ENJOY MOST

C hildren love to help in the kitchen, particularly on baking day, but to prevent disasters a little organization on your part will make things run much more smoothly.

Before starting explain what they are going to bake and what equipment is needed. Get out all the necessary ingredients and clarify any danger points such as the use of the hob or oven. Of course you will be on hand to help!

Very important – don't be the mug that washes up. Clearing up is all part of the fun and then the children can sit down and tuck into their own goodies.

In this chapter are cakes suitable for children to make and also some special ones for birthday parties. Recipes such as the *Ice-Cream Cake* (page 106) or the *Speedy Baked Alaska* (page 76) are also ideal for parties.

BUNNY RABBIT BIRTHDAY CAKE

•

FOR THE CAKE
275 g (10 oz) soft margarine
275 g (10 oz) caster sugar
5 eggs
275 g (10 oz) self-raising flour
2 ½ teaspoons baking powder

FOR THE BUTTER CREAM
225 g (8 oz) soft butter or margarine
450 g (1 lb) icing sugar, sieved

FOR THE DECORATION
About 350 g (12 oz) desiccated coconut
Large cake board or foil-covered baking tray
Sweets for eyes, nose and whiskers (smarties, jelly tots and Liquorice Allsorts)

You can use this basic shape to make other animals, such as a cat, teddy bear, koala bear or an owl. Chocolate vermicelli can be used in place of the coconut, if preferred.

Pre-heat the oven to gas mark 4, 350°F (180°C). Grease and base line two 18-cm (7-inch) and one 20-cm (8-inch) sandwich cake tins with greased greaseproof paper.

Measure all the ingredients for the cake into a large bowl and beat well for about 2 minutes until blended and smooth. Divide the mixture between the cake tins and bake for about 25–30 minutes for the 18-cm (7-inch) cakes, and 30–35 minutes for the 20-cm (8-inch) cake. When cooked the cakes will be well risen and the tops should spring back when lightly pressed with a finger. Leave the cakes to cool in their tins for a few minutes then turn out, peel off the paper and finish cooling on a wire rack.

Meanwhile, make up the butter cream by mixing the butter or margarine and icing sugar thoroughly together. Toast three quarters of the coconut until golden brown.

To make the rabbit shape, one of the 18-cm (7-inch) cakes is cut to form the ears, paws and tail. For the ears, cut 2 oval pieces from each side of the cake and then 1 smaller oval to form the hind paw and a circle for the tail (see Diagram 1).

Assemble the rabbit on the cake board using the 20-cm (8-inch) cake for the body and the remaining small cake for the head. Position the ears, paws and tail (see Diagram 2). Cover with the butter cream then sprinkle all over with the toasted coconut except the tail, inner ear and tummy. Use the untoasted coconut to define the inner ear, tummy and to cover the tail. Finish by adding the sweets for the eyes, nose and whiskers.

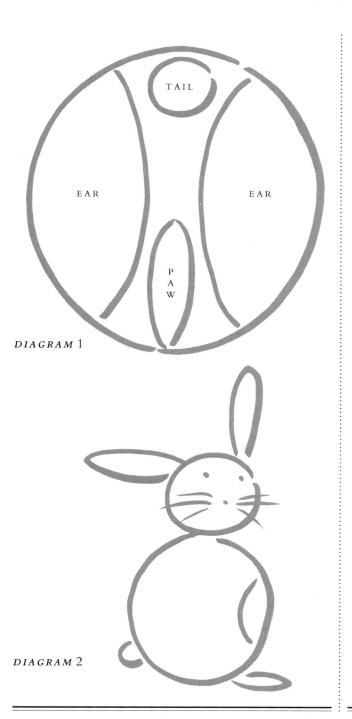

DIAGRAM 1

DIAGRAM 2

LITTLE GEMS

MAKES

—— 65 ——

INGREDIENTS

75 g (3 oz) soft margarine
2 eggs
100 g (4 oz) self-raising
  flour
1 teaspoon baking powder
75 g (3 oz) caster sugar
1 tablespoon milk

FOR THE DECORATION

100 g (4 oz) icing sugar,
  sieved
About 1 tablespoon lemon
  juice
About 65 jelly tots or
  Smarties

Children love to help by putting their favourite sweets on top of these tiny cakes. Sixty-five sounds like so many cakes but these are very tiny as they are made in sweetie or *petits fours* cases.

Pre-heat the oven to gas mark 4, 350°F (180°C). Arrange about 65 *petits fours* cases on baking trays.

Measure all the cake ingredients into a bowl and beat well until thoroughly blended. Spoon scant teaspoonfuls of the mixture into the cases being careful not to overfill.

Bake for about 15–20 minutes until well risen and pale golden brown. Cool on a wire rack.

For the icing: measure the icing sugar into a bowl and add sufficient lemon juice to give a spreading consistency. Spoon a little on top of each cake and spread out with the back of a teaspoon. When the icing has almost set, top with a Smartie or jelly tot.

ICED ANIMAL BISCUITS

M A K E S

—— about 50 ——

L et the children ice the animals themselves with their favourite colours. Animal cutters are available from good cook shops.

Pre-heat the oven to gas mark 5, 375°F (190°C). Lightly grease 2 baking trays.

Rub the fat into the flour until the mixture resembles fine breadcrumbs. Add the vanilla essence, sugar, beaten egg and milk to form a fairly stiff dough.

Roll out thinly on a lightly floured work surface, and cut into animal shapes using the cutters. Place on the baking trays and bake for 10–15 minutes until golden brown. Cool on a wire rack.

Measure the icing sugar into a bowl and add enough lemon juice to give a spreading consistency. Divide the icing into 2–3 small bowls (cups would do) and add a drop of different food colourings to each bowl, mixing well. Spoon a little icing onto each of the biscuits and spread out with the back of the teaspoon. Finish by adding silver balls for eyes.

INGREDIENTS

100 g (4 oz) butter, softened
225 g (8 oz) self-raising
 flour
Few drops vanilla essence
100 g (4 oz) caster sugar
1 egg, beaten
1 tablespoon milk

FOR THE ICING

100 g (4 oz) icing sugar,
 sieved
About 1 tablespoon lemon
 juice
Food colouring (red, green,
 blue, yellow)
Silver balls for eyes

JAMMY BUNS

M A K E S

—— 12 ——

225 g (8 oz) self-raising
  flour
Pinch of mixed spice
50 g (2 oz) margarine
50 g (2 oz) caster sugar
1 egg, beaten
About 3–4 tablespoons milk
Strawberry jam
Granulated sugar for dusting

Use your favourite jam for these and eat them as fresh as possible. A pinch of spice will add a little flavour to the recipe, but it'll be great fun for the children.

Pre-heat the oven to gas mark 6, 400°F (200°C). Grease a large baking tray.

Put the flour, spice and margarine into a bowl and rub in the margarine until the mixture resembles fine breadcrumbs. Stir in the sugar.

Blend the egg with the milk and stir gradually into the mixture, adding sufficient liquid to make a stiff dough. Divide the mixture into 12 pieces and roll into smooth balls. Make a hole in the centre of each with the handle of a wooden spoon and put about ½ teaspoon of jam into each one, then pinch the opening firmly together.

Turn the buns over and place, jam side-down, on the baking tray. Sprinkle them with a little granulated sugar and then bake for about 10–15 minutes until they are pale golden brown. Lift off the tray to cool a little on a wire rack. Serve while still warm.

COCONUT HAYSTACKS

M A K E S

—— about 6 ——

One of the easiest cakes for children to make. You don't have to use a mould, children have lots of fun moulding the haystacks by hand!

Pre-heat the oven to gas mark 4, 350°F (180°C). Place a sheet of non-stick baking parchment onto a baking tray.

Put the coconut and sugar in a bowl and mix together. Beat in sufficient egg to bind the mixture together but keeping it firm and add a few drops of pink colouring if wished.

Dip a small conical mould or an egg cup into cold water and drain it well. Fill with the coconut mixture and press down lightly. Turn the mould out onto the baking tray. Continue with the remaining mixture.

Bake for about 20 minutes or until the haystacks are tinged a pale golden brown. Lift off the baking tray and leave to cool on a wire rack.

INGREDIENTS

100g (4oz) desiccated coconut
50g (2oz) caster sugar
1 egg, beaten
A little pink food colouring (optional)

JUMBLES

M A K E S

—— 32 ——

150 g (5 oz) soft margarine
150 g (5 oz) caster sugar
Few drops vanilla essence
Finely grated rind of 1
*   lemon*
1 egg
350 g (12 oz) plain flour
Clear honey to glaze
Demerara sugar for dusting

I t is usual to shape this mixture into an 's', but of course you can shape it into any letter or number of your own choice.

Pre-heat the oven to gas mark 5, 375°F (190°C). Lightly grease 3 baking trays.

Measure all of the ingredients except the honey and demerara sugar into a bowl and work together by hand until a dough is formed. This can also be done in a food processor or with an electric mixer.

Divide the dough into 32 pieces. Roll each piece of dough into a strip about 10 cm (4 inches) long, then twist them into 's' shapes. Place on the baking trays and chill for about 30 minutes.

Bake for about 10–15 minutes until a pale golden colour. Remove from the oven. Turn the oven up to gas mark 8, 450°F (230°C) and while the jumbles are still warm, brush them well with honey and sprinkle with the demerara sugar. Return to the oven for 2–3 minutes until the sugar has caramelized. Cool on a wire rack.

BUTTERFLY CAKES

M A K E S

—— about 18 ——

Very traditional but still very popular and very quick to make.

Pre-heat the oven to gas mark 6, 400°F (200°C). Set about 18 paper cake cases into bun tins.

Measure all of the ingredients for the cake together in a bowl and beat well for 2–3 minutes until they are well blended and smooth. Divide the mixture between the paper cases and bake for about 15 minutes until the cakes are well risen and golden brown. Lift out and cool on a wire rack.

Meanwhile mix together the butter or margarine and icing sugar for the butter cream.

When the cakes are cold, cut a slice from the top of each one and cut this slice in half. Spoon a swirl of butter cream into the centre of the cakes and replace the 2 half slices of the cake into the icing, butterfly fashion. Dust with a little icing sugar.

INGREDIENTS

100 g (4 oz) soft margarine
100 g (4 oz) caster sugar
100 g (4 oz) self-raising flour
2 eggs
1 teaspoon baking powder

FOR THE BUTTER CREAM

100 g (4 oz) soft butter or margarine
225 g (8 oz) icing sugar, sieved

CHOCOLATE CRISPIES

MAKES

—— about 14 ——

INGREDIENTS

100 g (4 oz) margarine
2 tablespoons cocoa, sieved
2 rounded tablespoons golden
  syrup
65 g (2 ½ oz) cornflakes

E asy for children to make themselves, and always very popular. Use whatever cereal you have in the cupboard. If possible, make these on the day as they soon lose their crispness, although children don't seem to notice!

Melt the margarine in a fairly large saucepan, then stir in the cocoa and golden syrup. Mix well and remove from the heat. Add the cornflakes and mix gently until all the flakes are thoroughly covered.

Spoon into paper cake cases and leave to set for about 30 minutes until hard.

WHOLEFOOD CAKES

Oats, banana chips, carrots, nuts and brown flour add an extra dimension to baking both in flavour and texture. These recipes are delicious and particularly filling but more liquid and raising agent is usually needed in them as brown self-raising flour is more absorbent than white.

If you bake one of these cakes for Sunday tea and there's still half left afterwards, divide it into portions and freeze them. They're then ready to take out for lunch-boxes or picnics.

Remember, if you're trying to cut out calories you don't have to cut out cakes. Just make them with no icing and serve in smaller slices.

WHOLEMEAL GINGER CAKE

——— • ———

INGREDIENTS

175 g (6 oz) soft margarine
350 g (12 oz) golden syrup
120 g (4 ½ oz) granulated
  sugar
1 ½ tablespoons orange
  marmalade
200 ml (7 fl oz) milk
175 g (6 oz) self-raising
  white flour
1 ½ teaspoons ground ginger
1 ½ teaspoons ground mixed
  spice
½ teaspoon bicarbonate of
  soda
175 g (6 oz) self-raising
  brown flour
3 eggs, beaten

FOR THE ICING

About 3 tablespoons lemon
  juice
225 g (8 oz) icing sugar,
  sieved
Stem ginger to decorate
  (optional)

D on't be over-generous with the marmalade otherwise
the cake will sink!

Pre-heat the oven to gas mark 3, 325°F (160°C). Grease and
base line a roasting tin about 30 × 23 cm (12 × 9 inches)
with greased greaseproof paper.

Gently heat the margarine, syrup, sugar, marmalade and
milk together in a saucepan until the sugar has dissolved.
Allow to cool a little.

Sift the white self-raising flour with the spices and bicarbonate of soda into a mixing bowl. Add the brown flour and
mix together.

Stir the melted margarine and syrup mixture into the flours
with the beaten eggs. Stir well to form a smooth batter. Pour
into the prepared tin and bake for about 1 ½ hours or until it has
shrunk slightly from the sides of the tin and is springy to the
touch. Turn out and cool on a wire rack.

For the icing: mix together the lemon juice and icing sugar
and beat until smooth. Spread out evenly over the cake and
leave to set. Decorate with chopped stem ginger if liked.

CARROT CAKE

— • —

Sometimes known as passion cake – it's very naughty really but once in a while why not? To speed things up you could grate the carrots in a food processor.

Pre-heat the oven to gas mark 4, 350°F (180°C). Grease and line a deep 20-cm (8-inch) round cake tin with greased greaseproof paper.

Place all the ingredients for the cake except the almonds, walnuts, carrots and egg whites into a large bowl. Mix together for about 2 minutes until smooth and thoroughly blended.

Fold in the almonds and walnuts. Whisk the egg whites until stiff but not dry and fold into the mixture with the grated carrots.

Spoon the mixture into the prepared tin and bake for about 1 ½ hours until well risen and firm to the touch. Cover the cake with foil after 1 hour if the cake is becoming too brown. Leave to cool in the tin for a few minutes then turn out, remove the paper and leave to cool completely.

For the topping: beat together the cheese, honey and lemon juice and spread over the top of the cake. Sprinkle over the walnuts to decorate.

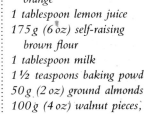

INGREDIENTS

225 g (8 oz) soft margarine
225 g (8 oz) light
    muscovado sugar
4 eggs, separated
Finely grated rind of ½
    orange
1 tablespoon lemon juice
175 g (6 oz) self-raising
    brown flour
1 tablespoon milk
1 ½ teaspoons baking powder
50 g (2 oz) ground almonds
100 g (4 oz) walnut pieces,
    chopped
350 g (12 oz) carrots, peeled
    and grated

FOR THE TOPPING
225 g (8 oz) low-fat soft
    cheese
2 teaspoons clear honey
1 teaspoon lemon juice
Chopped walnuts to decorate

FARMHOUSE ORANGE VICTORIA SANDWICH

———— • ————

Very special and beautifully moist.

Pre-heat the oven to gas mark 4, 350°F (180°C). Grease and base line two 18-cm (7-inch) sandwich cake tins with greased greaseproof paper.

Measure all the ingredients for the cake into a bowl and beat well for about 2 minutes, until smooth and blended. Divide the mixture between the 2 tins and level out evenly.

Bake for about 25–30 minutes, or until the cakes have shrunk away slightly from the sides of the tin, and will spring back when lightly pressed with a finger. Turn the cakes out onto a wire rack to cool and peel off the paper.

Measure the ingredients for the filling into a bowl and blend together until smooth. Use to sandwich the cakes together. Dust the top of the cake with sieved icing sugar.

INGREDIENTS

175 g (6 oz) soft margarine
175 g (6 oz) light
  muscovado sugar
3 eggs
175 g (6 oz) self-raising
  brown flour
1 ½ teaspoons baking powder
Grated rind of 1 orange
2 tablespoons milk

FOR THE FILLING
40 g (1 ½ oz) soft margarine
100 g (4 oz) icing sugar,
  sieved
1–2 tablespoons fine-cut
  marmalade

TO FINISH
Icing sugar, sieved

OAT AND SUNFLOWER SQUARES

M A K E S
—— about 16 ——

T ry to use the jumbo oats which are available from health food stores as these give a crunchier texture than porridge oats.

———————

Pre-heat the oven to gas mark 4, 350°F (180°C). Lightly grease a shallow 18-cm (7-inch) square tin.

Heat the margarine and syrup until evenly blended. Mix the oats and sunflower seeds together in a bowl and pour on the syrup mixture. Stir thoroughly to mix. Spoon into the prepared tin and press the mixture down well with the back of a spoon.

Bake for about 20–25 minutes or until golden brown and just firm to the touch. Cut into squares and then allow to cool in the tin before carefully lifting out.

INGREDIENTS

50 g (2 oz) margarine
2 rounded tablespoons golden syrup
150 g (5 oz) jumbo oats
50 g (2 oz) sunflower seeds

MUESLI BISCUITS

M A K E S

—— about 18 ——

INGREDIENTS

100 g (4 oz) soft margarine
50 g (2 oz) demerara sugar
1 tablespoon clear honey
50 g (2 oz) self-raising
  brown flour
175 g (6 oz) muesli
1 egg

Good with morning coffee. You can vary the flavour of these biscuits by using different types of muesli.

Pre-heat the oven to gas mark 5, 375°F (190°C). Lightly grease 2 baking trays.

Cream together the margarine and sugar. Mix in the remaining ingredients to form a firm dough.

Roll the mixture into balls about the size of a walnut. Place well apart on the baking trays and flatten slightly with the palm of the hand.

Bake for about 15 minutes or until crisp and golden brown. Carefully lift off and leave to cool on a wire rack.

CRACKERJACKS

M A K E S

—— about 36 ——

I've been making these since my own children were small. They never seem to turn out exactly the same as the syrup varies just a little.

Pre-heat the oven to gas mark 4, 350°F (180°C). Lightly grease 2 baking trays.

Measure the margarine, syrup and sugar into a pan and heat gently until melted. Stir in the remaining ingredients. Mix well until blended then spoon about 36 slightly flattened mounds well apart on the baking trays.

Bake for about 10 minutes, until they have spread out flat and are lightly browned at the edges. Leave to cool on the trays for a few moments. Carefully lift off with a palette knife and finish cooling on a wire rack.

INGREDIENTS

150 g (5 oz) soft margarine
1 rounded tablespoon golden syrup
175 g (6 oz) golden granulated sugar
75 g (3 oz) self-raising flour
75 g (3 oz) desiccated coconut
100 g (4 oz) porridge oats

LEMON REFRIGERATOR BISCUITS

M A K E S
—— about 32 ——

150 g (5 oz) butter, softened
150 g (5 oz) caster sugar
Grated rind of 2 lemons
1 egg
225 g (8 oz) plain flour
Demerara sugar for rolling

You could use chopped nuts or rolled oats in place of the demerara sugar for a change.

Lightly grease 2 baking trays.

Measure the butter, caster sugar, lemon rind, egg and flour into a bowl and mix together until a dough is formed. (Use a food processor if you like.) Knead the dough lightly then wrap and chill in the refrigerator for about 30 minutes.

Roll the dough into a sausage shape about 5 cm (2 inches) in diameter and 20 cm (8 inches) long. Wrap in greaseproof paper and chill again for about 30 minutes.

Pre-heat the oven to gas mark 5, 375°F (190°C). Roll the dough in the demerara sugar, then cut into 5-mm (¼-inch) slices. Place on the baking trays.

Bake for about 12–15 minutes or until golden. Lift off the trays and cool on a wire rack.

BANANA CHIP BARS

MAKES

—— 12 ——

A really healthy snack. The banana in the middle could be replaced with ready-soaked apricots.

———

Pre-heat the oven to gas mark 4, 350°F (180°C). Lightly grease a shallow 18-cm (7-inch) square tin.

Mix together the flour, oats and sugar in a bowl. Rub in the fat until the mixture resembles breadcrumbs. Spread half of the mixture over the base of the tin and arrange the sliced banana on top. Sprinkle over the remaining crumb mixture and press down well. Top with the banana chips.

Bake for about 25 minutes or until golden brown. Leave in the tin until cold and then cut into bars to serve.

INGREDIENTS

75g (3 oz) self-raising brown flour
75g (3 oz) rolled oats
75g (3 oz) demerara sugar
100g (4 oz) margarine
1 ripe banana, sliced
25g (1 oz) banana chips

INDEX

Entries in *italic* refer to illustrations

A

All-Bran Fruit Loaf	21
all-in-one method	12
Almond Cheesecake Tartlets	91
Almond and chocolate chip cake	36
Almond Spice Cake	32
American Chocolate Muffins	59
Apricot and Orange Hob-Nob Cheesecake	83, 88

B

Baked Alaska, Speedy	75, 76, 113
Bakewell Tart Traybake	98
baking powder	8–9, 14
Banana Chip Bars	131
Banana Loaf Cake	50
bars	12, 112, 131
Biscuits and cookies	37–44
Cheesy Biscuits, Rich	44
Chocolate Chip Cookies	42, 67
Cornish Fairings	38
Flapjacks, Fast	41
Melting Moments	40
Shortbread, The Very Best	43, 67
Shrewsbury Biscuits	39
Black Forest Cake	56
'Boozy' Fruit Cake	51
Borrowdale Tea Bread	22, *33*
Brandy Chocolate Charlotte	82
Breads and teabreads, quick	12, 17–24
All-Bran Fruit Loaf	21
Borrowdale Tea Bread	22, *33*
Cheese and Celery Crown Loaf	24
English Muffins	19
Granary Rolls, Quick	18
Irish Soda Bread	20
Sultana Malt Loaf	23
Bunny Rabbit Birthday Cake	114–15

butter	8, 12
Butterfly Cakes	121

C

Cakes for dessert	75–82
Baked Alaska, Speedy	76
Brandy Chocolate Charlotte	82
Ginger Cream Roll	81
Guernsey Apple Cake	78
Raspberry Meringue Roulade	75, 79
Strawberry Pavlova	80
Tiramisu	*68–9*, 77
Cakes that children enjoy most	113–22
Bunny Rabbit Birthday Cake	114–15
Butterfly Cakes	˙121
Chocolate Crispies	122
Coconut Haystacks	119
Iced Animal Biscuits	117
Jammy Buns	118
Jumbles	120
Little Gems	116
candied peel	10
Carrot Cake	125
Cheese and Celery Crown Loaf	24
Cheesecakes, fast	12, 83–91
Almond Cheesecake Tartlets	91
Apricot and Orange Hob-Nob Cheesecake	83, 88
Chocolate, Rum and Raisin Cheesecake	89
Continental Cheesecake	87
German Cheesecake	86
Laura's American Cheesecake	84
Lemon Cheesecake, Easy	85
Lime Cheesecake	92
Orange Jaffa Cheesecake	90, *103*
Cheesy Biscuits, Rich	44

cherries, glacé	10
Cherry and Apricot Traybake	99
cherry cakes	12
Cherry Loaf Cake	26
chocolate	9, 53
piping	15
Chocolate cakes	46, 53–61
American Chocolate Muffins	59
Black Forest Cake	56
Chocolate Chip Brownies	55
Chocolate Eclairs	62
Chocolate Fudge Cake	60
Chocolate Roulade	57
Date and Chocolate Loaf	54
Devil's Food Cake	61
Double Chocolate Cookies	58
Chocolate Chip Brownies	55
Chocolate Chip Cookies	42, 67
Chocolate Crispies	122
Chocolate eclairs	62
Chocolate Fudge Cake	60
Chocolate Marble Traybake	96
Chocolate Roulade	57
Chocolate, Rum and Raisin Cheesecake	89
Chocolate Terrine	107
Christmas Cake, Quick	35
Coconut Haystacks	119
Coffee Cake	46
Coffee Fudge Squares	101
Coffee and Walnut Sponge Cake	31
Continental Cheesecake	87
Cornish Fairings	38
Crackerjacks	67, 129
Cut and Come Again Cake	47

D

Date and Chocolate Loaf	54
Devil's Food Cake	61
Double Chocolate Cookies	58
Dundee Cake	27

E

eggs	9
English Muffins	19
equipment	11–12

F

Family cakes	**45–52**
Banana Loaf Cake	50
'Boozy' Fruit Cake	51
Chocolate Cake	46
Coffee Cake	46
Cut and Come Again Cake	47
Ginger and Orange Cake, Sticky	48
Orange or Lemon Cake	46
Seed Cake, Old-fashioned	52
Victoria Sandwich Cake, All-In-One	46
WI Mincemeat Loaf Cakes	49
Farmhouse Orange Victoria Sandwich	*104*, 126
Filo Apple Strudels	*70*, 74
Flapjacks, Fast	12, 41
flour	8
self-raising	14
food processor	11
freezing	16
fruit cakes	12, 16
fruit, dried	9
Fruit Scones, Special	73
Fruit Traybake	100

G

gelatine	10, 83
German Cheesecake	86
Ginger Cake, Wholemeal	124
Ginger Cream Roll	81
Ginger and Orange Cake, Sticky	48
gingerbread	16
golden syrup	10
Granary Rolls, Quick	18
Guernsey Apple Cake	78

H

Honey Fudge Wedges	110

I

Ice-Cream Cake	106, 113
Iced Animal Biscuits	117
Iced Chocolate Traybake	97
Iced Krispie Bars	112
Iced Lemon Traybake	95
ingredients	8–10
Irish Soda Bread	20

J

Jammy Buns	118
Jumbles	120

L

Large cakes and sponge cakes	**25–35**
Almond and chocolate chip cake	36
Almond Spice Cake	32
Cherry Loaf Cake	26
Christmas Cake, Quick	35
Coffee and Walnut Sponge Cake	31
Dundee Cake	27
Pineapple and Sultana Cake	30, *34*
Swiss Roll	12, 28–9
Laura's American Cheesecake	84
Lemon Buns, Crusty	64
Lemon Cheesecake, Easy	85
lemon juice	9
Lemon Refrigerator Biscuits	130
Lime cheesecake	92
lining tins	12, 13–14
Little cakes and scones	**63–74**
Filo Apple Strudels	*70*, 74
Fruit Scones, Special	73
Lemon Buns, Crusty	64
Rock Cakes, Mini	66
Scotch Pancakes	71
Swiss Cakes	65
Welsh Cakes	72
Little Gems	116

M

margarine	8, 12
Melting Moments	40
Mincemeat and Almond Bake	102
Muesli Biscuits	128

N

No-bake cakes	**105–12**
Chocolate Terrine	107
Honey Fudge Wedges	110
Ice-Cream Cake	106, 113
Iced Krispie Bars	112
Nut and Sultana Tiffin	109
Passion Sponge	111
Toffee and Marshmallow Squares	108
Nut and Sultana Tiffin	109
nuts	9
toasting	16

O

Oat and Sunflower Squares	127
Orange Jaffa Cheesecake	90, *103*
Orange or Lemon Cake	46
ovens	12

P

palette knife	11
Passion Sponge	111
Pineapple and Sultana Cake	30, *34*
piping	15

Q

raising agents	8–9
raspberries	75
Raspberry Meringue Roulade	75, 79
Rock Cakes, Mini	66

S

Scotch Pancakes	71
scrapers	11
Seed Cake, Old-fashioned	52
Shortbread, The Very Best	43, *67*
Shrewsbury Biscuits	39
spices	10
sponge cakes	12, 16
Sponge Traybake, Basic All-In-One	94
storing	16
Strawberry Pavlova	75, 80
sugar	9
Sultana Malt Loaf	23
Swiss Cakes	65
Swiss Roll	12, 28
Chocolate	29
Coffee	29
Lemon	29
Orange	29
Raspberry or Strawberry	29

T

testing   14
tins and trays   11–12
Tiramisu   *68–9*, 75, 77
toffee   12
Toffee and Marshmallow Squares   108
Traybakes   12, *68–9*, 93–102
  Bakewell Tart Traybake   98
  Cherry and Apricot Traybake   99
  Chocolate Marble Traybake   96
  Coffee Fudge Squares   101
  Fruit Traybake   100
  Iced Chocolate Traybake   97
  Iced Lemon Traybake   95
  Mincemeat and Almond Bake   102

Sponge Traybake, Basic All-In-One   94
treacle, black   10

V

Victoria Sandwich Cake, All-In-One   46

W

Welsh Cakes   72
whisk   11
Wholefood cakes   123–31
  Banana Chip Bars   131
  Carrot Cake   125
  Crackerjacks   *67*, 129
  Farmhouse Orange Victoria Sandwich   *104*, 126
  Ginger Cake, Wholemeal   124
  Lemon Refrigerator Biscuits   130
  Muesli Biscuits   128
  Oat and Sunflower Squares   127
WI Mincemeat Loaf Cakes   49

Y

yeast, easy-blend dried   10
Yorkshire Parkin   16

BBC BOOKS · *Quick & Easy Cookery Series*

Launched in 1989 by Ken Hom and Sarah Brown, the *Quick & Easy* Cookery series is a culinary winner. Everything about the titles is aimed at quick and easy recipes – the ingredients, the cooking methods and the author's techniques and tips. Eight pages of colour photographs are also included to provide a flash of inspiration for the frantic or faint-hearted.

Other titles already published:

Beverley Piper's Quick & Easy Healthy Cookery
Clare Connery's Quick & Easy Salads
Joanna Farrow's Quick & Easy Fish Cookery
Ken Hom's Quick & Easy Chinese Cookery
Madhur Jaffrey's Quick & Easy Indian Cookery
Sandeep Chatterjee's Quick & Easy Indian Vegetarian Cookery
Sarah Brown's Quick & Easy Vegetarian Cookery
Shaun Hill's Quick & Easy Vegetable Cookery

Titles to come:

Joanna Farrow's Quick & Easy Cake Decorating
Linda Fraser's Quick & Easy Suppers
Simone Sekers' Quick & Easy Preserves
Thane Prince's Quick & Easy Soups